Hannah

History

History
TODAY

Anne Boleyn
One short life that changed the English-speaking world

Colin Hamer

DayOne

© Day One Publications 2007
First printed 2007

ISBN 978-1-84625-083-5

ISBN 978-1-84625-083-5

British Library Cataloguing in Publication Data available

Published by Day One Publications
Ryelands Road, Leominster, HR6 8NZ
☎ 01568 613 740 FAX 01568 611 473
email—sales@dayone.co.uk
web site—www.dayone.co.uk
North American—e-mail—sales@dayonebookstore.com
North American—web site—www.dayonebookstore.com

Cover design by Wayne McMaster
Designed by Steve Devane and printed by Gutenberg Press, Malta

While William Tyndale was praying in his dying moments that God would open the eyes of the King of England, God had already answered the prayer in his own way: he had used a woman to influence the King and the nation with the gospel of salvation through Jesus Christ. That woman was Anne Boleyn, and in this fascinating biography of her short life, Colin Hamer skilfully shows how God prepared Anne for this important work and used her to bring Reformed truth into the powerhouse of England.

For those a little confused about the wives of Henry VIII and particularly the role of Anne Boleyn, this book is very helpful. It also brings the challenge to all Christian believers to live for God wherever they are.

Kath Dredge, Further Education tutor and manager of Hall Green BookPoint, Haworth, and author of Living4God: Learning from the lives of William Tyndale, John Newton, David Brainerd and Eric Liddell.

Colin Hamer's Anne Boleyn is as exciting as fiction as it carefully makes its way through the historical and religious complexities of Henry VIII's England. Far more important than simply as one of the six wives of Henry, Anne was an influential figure in her own right, strengthening the King's determination to break with Rome and encouraging her country's move toward Protestantism by her own convictions and her public courage and tenacity. Very much a woman of her times, with strengths and flaws, Anne Boleyn became in her short life not only Queen of England but one of the makers of English history.

David B. Calhoun, Professor of Church History at Covenant Theological Seminary, St Louis, Missouri, and author of books on church history, including a two-volume history of Princeton Seminary (Banner of Truth) and Grace Abounding: The Life, Books and Influence of John Bunyan (Christian Focus).

Colin Hamer's new book is a spirited and engaging biography of the beautiful, dark-eyed Anne Boleyn, second of Henry VIII's six wives. What makes this treatment so fascinating is that Hamer rightly understands her important (one might say vital) role in support of the 'new learning'—Protestantism. As Henry's queen, Anne brought her evangelical convictions (learned from Marguerite d'Angoulême) to Henry's Tudor court where she worked clandestinely as an advocate for the Protestant cause. The story told

Commendations

here makes for a stimulating read and will give the reader a deeper and richer understanding of the English Reformation.

Frank A. James III, President and Professor of Historical Theology, Reformed Theological Seminary, Orlando, Florida, USA

For Rosina Ferdinand

Who has made her life count for God

Contents

Contents

Acknowledgements

I would like to thank Sharon Syers, Liz Jackman, Digby James and Suzanne Mitchell for their encouragement, helpful comments and work on the manuscript.

Any search of the Internet will reveal many biographies of Anne Boleyn, but on closer inspection most are like the drama documentaries of television today—works of fiction that build loosely on the facts. They usually perpetuate the myth that Anne Boleyn was an immoral woman who seduced Henry VIII away from his rightful wife for the advancement of her family and personal gain. The year 2004 saw the publication of two biographies that set the record straight—one by Eric Ives and the other by Joanna Denny.

This book is not an attempt to repeat the work of these two historians, but instead to set Anne Boleyn in her context as a young woman who had come to faith in Christ, and was then thrust into the highest echelons of Tudor power politics in turbulent times. It will endeavour to explore the consequent impact on Henry VIII's policies and the course of the English Reformation.

Anne Boleyn's life is an exciting story. These were difficult and 'messy' times; often there appeared to be no clear answers to the pressing questions of the day.

Let us be challenged and encouraged by the fact that this one short life came to have a huge impact on subsequent generations throughout the world.

Timeline

1491	June 28	Henry VIII born
1501		**Anne Boleyn born**
	November 14	Catherine of Aragon marries Arthur, Henry VII's eldest son
1502	April 2	Arthur dies
1509	April 12	Henry VIII crowned
	June 11	Henry VIII marries Catherine of Aragon
1511		Thomas Wolsey becomes a member of the Privy Council
1513		**Anne goes abroad to the court of Margaret of Austria**
1514		**Anne goes to the French court and meets Marguerite d'Angoulême**
1515	September 10	Thomas Wolsey appointed a cardinal by the Pope
	December 24	Thomas Wolsey appointed Lord Chancellor
1516	February 18	Catherine gives birth to Mary—the future Mary I
1517		Thomas More becomes a member of the Privy Council
	October 31	Martin Luther objects to Catholic teaching and practice
1521	October 11	Henry VIII declared defender of the Catholic faith by the Pope
	December	**Anne returns to England**
1522	**March 4**	**Anne performs in the mock castle raid at the Tudor court**
1523		**Henry Percy wants to marry Anne—she is sent to Hever**
1524		Henry VIII ceases his sexual relationship with Catherine
1525	June	Henry VIII takes steps to make Henry Fitzroy heir to the throne
1526		**Henry VIII notices Anne and tells Thomas Wyatt to stay away**
		The great 'divorce' debate starts
1527	June	Henry tells Catherine he wants an annulment of their marriage
	July 1	**Anne sends Henry a gift signifying she accepts him as a suitor**
1529	**May/June**	**Legatine court to decide the annulment fails to reach a conclusion**
	October 9	Cardinal Wolsey charged with praemunire
		Anne now the most influential figure at court
		Thomas More appointed Lord Chancellor
		Thomas Cranmer comes to the King's attention
		Chapuys is appointed imperial ambassador
1530	November 29	Cardinal Wolsey dies
1531		Thomas Cromwell becomes a member of the Privy Council
		Henry VIII officially separates from Catherine of Aragon
1532	**October 11**	**Anne and Henry travel to France to meet Francis I**
	November 14	**Anne marries Henry at a secret ceremony in Dover**

1533	January 25	**Anne and Henry go through another wedding ceremony in London**
		Thomas Cromwell is appointed Lord Chancellor
	March 30	Thomas Cranmer is appointed Archbishop of Canterbury
	May 23	Catherine's marriage to Henry VIII is annulled
	June 1	**Anne is crowned queen**
	September 7	**Anne gives birth to Elizabeth—the future Elizabeth I**
1534		**Anne's next baby is stillborn**
1535	July 6	Thomas More is executed
	September 19	The evangelicals Foxe, Latimer, and Hilsey consecrated as bishops
1536	January 7	Catherine of Aragon dies
	January 29	**Anne miscarries**
	April 2	John Skip preaches a controversial sermon
	May 2	**Anne is arrested and taken to the Tower**
	May 15	**Anne is tried for treason and found guilty**
	May 17	**Anne's 'accomplices' are executed**
		Anne's marriage to Henry VIII is annulled
	May 19	**Anne Boleyn is executed**
	May 20	Henry VIII is betrothed to Jane Seymour
	May 30	Henry VIII marries Jane Seymour
	October 6	William Tyndale is martyred
1537	October 12	Edward VI born
	October 24	Jane Seymour dies
1540	January 6	Henry VIII marries Anne of Cleves
	July 9	Marriage to Anne of Cleves is annulled
	July 28	Henry VIII marries Catherine Howard
	July 28	Thomas Cromwell is executed
1542	February 13	Catherine Howard is executed
1543	July 12	Henry VIII marries Katherine Parr
1547	January 28	Henry VIII dies, succeeded by Edward VI
1553	July 6	Edward VI dies. Mary I becomes queen
1558	November 17	Mary I dies. Elizabeth I (Anne Boleyn's daughter) becomes queen
1603	March 24	Elizabeth I dies and the Tudor dynasty ends

Introduction

Anne Boleyn, twenty years old, stepped onto the shore at Dover in the winter of 1521 after several years abroad. She had been sent to France to assimilate French culture and language—which were all the fashion at the English court. Anne's father, Sir Thomas Boleyn,[1] was a diplomat, linguist, sportsman, expert in law—and a member of Henry VIII's close circle of courtiers. He was ambitious for his daughter to be favourably placed in the marriage market of the time; she was to be a debutante at the Tudor court—it would be all extravagant banquets, fine clothes, dancing, and much revelry.

Anne had used her time abroad well. According to her contemporaries she was a brilliant, vivacious, sharp-witted young woman who spoke French as if it was her mother tongue. She had completely mastered French culture, manners, and dress code. She was all set to make a big impression at court—and did. As was observed at the time by Lancelot de Carles, a Spaniard who acted as secretary to the French ambassador at the Tudor court, she stood out from the other women—'For her behaviour, manners, attire and tongue she excelled them all'[2]—wearing at the New Year celebrations a yellow satin gown and caul (a close-fitting headdress) of Venetian gold that was subject to special comment.

Henry VIII, however, was the real centre of attention. He was the archetypal kingly figure; reputedly handsome (at least in his youth), athletic, over six feet tall and with a large frame, he was imposing to look at. He saw himself as an intellectual, a musician, and a theologian. He loved to be the focus of attention, and hugely enjoyed the court life of eating, drinking, dancing, play-acting, hunting, and jousting.

Outside this heady world of King Henry VIII's court there were probably three million souls in England subsisting in a largely agrarian economy that had changed little in centuries. National life was dominated by a medieval Catholicism where superstition, the worship of idols and relics, widespread ignorance, and immorality were the order of the day—as has been acknowledged by historians even from within the Roman Catholic faith community.

What nobody could have predicted was that England was about to strike out in a dramatic new direction; the next 150 years would see the most momentous events in the nation's history—years that were subsequently labelled the English Reformation. Secular historians, particularly in the last thirty years or so, have argued about the true origins of these changes and the political and religious motivations of the period, but they do not dispute the chronology; in the years immediately following Anne Boleyn's arrival in England the settled religious life of the nation started to change.

Few eventful periods of history can be attributed to single issues or causes. Life is more complex than this—it rarely (from our human perspective at least) runs straight like an arrow to some predetermined goal. But with the hindsight of nearly 500 years and a mass of historical research at our disposal, it is difficult not to see that something Anne Boleyn brought with her in the winter of 1521 had a significance that totally eclipsed any expensive satin gown. All the evidence points to the fact that, in France, Anne had found a personal faith in Christ.

One hundred and fifty years earlier in England, John Wycliffe had discovered in the Bible (which he had translated into English from the Latin Vulgate version) the doctrines that most 'evangelical' Christians would subscribe to today.[3] But Wycliffe and his followers (known as Lollards) had failed to make much impact on national life. The Lollards had become isolated groups of believers scattered around the country, often persecuted for their beliefs. England was still a Catholic country.

But in 1517 Martin Luther[4] had set Europe aflame when he nailed his famous ninety-five theses on the door of the church of Wittenberg Castle in Germany outlining his objections to Catholic doctrine and practice. The European printing presses had burst into life producing the new evangelical books and tracts. While in France, Anne was a reader of this 'new learning' that was sweeping across Europe—literature that had to be smuggled into London as it had been banned as heretical.[5] Meanwhile William Tyndale[6] was meeting in the White Horse Inn at Cambridge with like-minded evangelicals; his writings, and particularly his published New Testament in English, the first from the Greek, would soon cause him to be branded a heretic by the Roman Catholic Church. Tyndale's career as translator, writer, and fugitive from his persecutors was about to begin.

Anne Boleyn had brought these banned books right into Henry VIII's court; it was not long before Henry VIII himself started to take note of this new phenomenon—both the woman and her 'new learning'. Within a few short years the die was cast; when Anne returned from a time away at the family home, Jean du Bellay, the French ambassador to the Tudor court, remarked, 'Mademoiselle Boulan (Boleyn) has returned to court. The King is so infatuated that none but God can cure him …'

There followed a rapidly unfolding sequence of events that set the course for England to become a home for the gospel for the benefit of the post-medieval world, a course that meant that this small country, in religion, politics, and trade, has had an influence far out of proportion to its geographical size or population for the last 500 years.

Notes

1 See Appendix 4: Biographical sketches.
2 **Denny,** p. 5.
3 An evangelical Christian is a Christian who gives ultimate authority to the Bible's teaching.
4 See Appendix 4: Biographical sketches.
5 'Heresy' was any teaching that contradicted the teachings of the Roman Catholic Church.
6 See Appendix 4: Biographical sketches.

Part 1

The Middle Ages

Which way heaven?

A lthough she was in the grave by the age of thirty-six, and on the throne of England for only three years (and that nearly 500 years ago), mention the name of Anne Boleyn today in any group of people and there will be a reaction from some. Why is this? Because she played a fundamental role in changing for millions the answer to the question—Which way heaven?

In 16th-century Europe there was a universal belief in heaven and hell— the debate was about how to reach one and avoid the other. In our modern Western world the afterlife might be an occasional and interesting dinner-table conversation, but back then your future destiny was all-important. More important, as Bill Shankly (former manager of Liverpool Football Club) once said, when speaking about football, than life and death.

For a thousand years Christendom believed what the Roman Catholic Church taught—that Christ's work on the cross, and all the favours of heaven, belonged to the Church; only the Church could administer the benefits of heaven through the sacramental system it had invented. These sacraments, it taught, were the means by which man received God's favour or 'grace', without which you were destined for hell.[1] Kings and queens, rich and poor, all had to come to the Church. Heaven was only entered through its gates; truly it had the keys to heaven and hell. And the issue went deeper. It did not affect only matters 'spiritual': the Church also believed that all earthly powers were ultimately subject to its authority.

In the year 1500 western Europe was still united in its Roman Catholicism—all paying homage to the pope at Rome. By the 1520s some German states were beginning to break away, but England, that distant outpost of Catholicism, remained loyal; indeed Henry VIII wrote a thesis in defence of the Church's teaching entitled *Assertion of the Seven Sacraments*, and was awarded the title 'Defender of the Faith' by the Pope in 1521, a title retained, ironically, right down to our own day by the British monarchy in its capacity as head of the Church of England. 1521 was the very year that Anne Boleyn returned to England from France bringing the heresy that Henry had condemned; by 1533 England had made its historic break from Rome—a move that rocked Christendom. How had this happened? Henry VIII needed to defy the pope to marry Anne Boleyn, and he used the new teachings she had brought from France to achieve it. In a sense England has stood apart from continental Europe ever since.

What was this new way to heaven? Many able scholars, as they gained access to the text of the Bible, saw that entry to heaven was based on Christ's merits alone, and freely accessible to every man, woman, and child, without any earthly organization or system to intervene; that the Christian life is a life marked out by obedience to God's commands as taught in the Bible, summarized by Christ as firstly, loving God, and secondly, loving your neighbour.

In contrast the Roman Church taught that entry to heaven was based on receiving grace through its sacraments. For Christians finally to achieve heaven they needed a constant supply of that grace, received principally by a continuous observance of the Church's rituals. Great emphasis was also put on the lives of 'saints'—these were people who had in the past lived exemplary lives and after death had been 'beatified' by the Church. These saints were to be prayed to in order that they might grant specific requests, the supreme saint being Jesus' mother, Mary—whose worship was (and is) actively encouraged by the Catholic Church.

Grace could also be dispensed at shrines. They often house at least one 'relic'—items that are believed to have come from a saint, or one of the original apostles, or even Christ himself. Listed among the relics at Bury St Edmunds in 1535 were the coals with which St Laurence was toasted, the parings of St Edmund's nails, and St Thomas of Canterbury's penknife. Some of the bread used to feed the five thousand was claimed to be at Peterborough, along with even a feather of Gabriel's wing. These were all thought to have a sort of 'magic' property, so to touch, or even see, such an item might 'confer grace'. The concept is apiece with the belief that when the bread and wine are consecrated by the priest in the Church service known as the Mass, they actually become the body and blood of Christ— the supreme 'relic' that confers grace. Pilgrimages are similarly part of the system that helps a person on the way to heaven—if a journey is made to some particular shrine, or to see some relic, grace is in some way credited to his or her account.

But it was the Church's practice of granting indulgences that was the spark to ignite the Reformation, as the movement against orthodox Catholic teaching came to be called. The Church believed that even when the sacramental system was carefully observed, on death, heaven was to be entered through a transitional phase—purgatory. In purgatory the remaining sin clinging to your life was 'purged' so that your soul would be sufficiently pure to enter heaven; the length of time you spent in this extremely unpleasant place depended on how much sin there was left to purge.

But there was hope of relief from this painful experience—you could call on the Church's saints for help to hasten your journey. Their 'excess' good works were deemed able to credit a kind of central spiritual merit account. The ordinary person could request that some of this merit be credited to his or her own, or someone else's, account; once in the specified account the pains of purgatory were eased for that person. When so applied the extra merit was called an indulgence. Who owned the merit account? It was, of course, the Church. It is not difficult to anticipate what happened next: the indulgence was sold by the Church, often to relatives, to ease the passing of a deceased loved one through purgatory.[2]

It was this practice that the monk and university lecturer Martin Luther took particular exception to, and his teachings (and that of other Reformers) began to spread widely. More and more people learned that the Church's system for reaching heaven was not in the Bible. They came across for the first time that foundational doctrine—'justification by faith'. They read that Christ had paid a sufficient sacrifice on Calvary's cross to pay for all sin. There was no purgatory. No further rituals, masses, penances—or even good works—were required to secure a place in heaven. All that any man, woman, or child needed was to receive by faith the gift of eternal life freely offered by Christ. Truly this was 'amazing grace': the demands of justice had been met by God himself. It is difficult to see how the Bible could have been clearer: 'For it is by grace you have been saved, through faith—and this not from yourselves, it is the gift of God—not by works, so that no one can boast.'[3] Individuals are brought into a loving relationship with God because he first loved them; in response to that love they, by faith, receive the forgiveness that Christ freely offers. Here is the gospel, hidden for so long.

Surely Zahl is right when he states: '... Catholicism sought to objectify, or make concrete and palpable, the relation between God and humanity. ... The relationship between God and humanity is, like all relationships in life, unseen ... [Catholicism was] a system of "meritorious" actions and offerings and indulgences and pilgrimages and prostrations that did not reflect the authentic inwardness of life and love.'[4]

This new teaching was described as 'new learning', what today would be described as 'evangelical'. People who held these views were often called 'Protestant', because they were seen to be protesting against Catholic teaching and practice. But it is not good for any group to be defined by what they do *not* believe in, and, what is more, Luther certainly did not simply protest against Catholicism, he fully grasped the wonder of the biblical gospel. His commentaries and hymns show this, including the following:

'Tis through thy love alone we gain
The pardon of our sin
The strictest life is but in vain,
Our works can nothing win ...
Wherefore my hope is in the Lord,
My works I count but dust
I build not there, but on his word
And in his goodness trust.[5]

Men and women could now have assurance of a life to come in heaven with their Saviour—based not on a creaking system of penances and good works of their own, or of some past saint, but rather on Jesus Christ's own blood and sinless life. People gained their assurance not from the Church, but from Christ himself—whom they could now read about for themselves in ever-increasing numbers as the Bible began to be translated into the vernacular: first into German by Luther, then soon after into English by, most notably, William Tyndale.

Not only did this effect a profound spiritual change in the lives of many individuals, but there was also a corresponding psychological impact— everybody was now potentially free of the Church's control. They could 'walk tall' as men or women before God. They did not have to fear alienating the local priest or the Church hierarchy, but could go about their daily tasks endeavouring to please their Saviour, not a system. Their soul's destiny was, in a sense, in their own hands, not in those of a 'foreign' potentate—as the Church had often seemed to be with its distant pope exercising ultimate control. Although the focus of most historical books has been necessarily on the more measurable impact of the Reformation on political and national life (and to an extent this book will be no exception), this new individual and personal dimension to faith also had an immense influence on the mindset of English people, a mindset they exported in many missionary endeavours in subsequent centuries, and which contributed much to making many English-speaking peoples what they are today.

At first the Church thought they could ignore Luther—there had been other heretics before and the Church had stood the test of time. But they had not counted on the 16th-century equivalent of the Internet age—the new German printing presses. The numbers holding to the new Reformed views rapidly increased; eventually the Church began to see a threat to its future. Its wealth and power base were rooted in its sacramental system and its claim to be able to intercede with God on man's behalf—in direct contradiction to the Bible, in which thousands could now read for themselves such statements as: 'For there is one God and one mediator between God and men, the man Christ Jesus.'[6]

The 'new learning' had laid an axe to the whole sacramental system. The scene was set for the religious (and consequently political) power struggles in England for the next 200 years; the subsequent changes have impacted national life right down to the 21st century.

It will be seen that Anne Boleyn, born at the dawn of what historians call the modern era, played a crucial role in this. But first an attempt will be made to catch a glimpse of her world—that lost world of medieval England.

Notes

1   See Appendix 2: The seven sacraments.

2   The Roman Catholic Church still believes in the whole system of indulgences; it is just the abuse of selling them that they have repudiated. See **Kreeft,** p. 346.

3   Ephesians 2:8–9.

4   **Zahl,** pp. 12–13.

5   **Rosman,** p. 20.

6   1 Timothy 2:5.

Life in the Middle Ages

I t is said that the past is a foreign country. If it was possible to take a time capsule trip back to early 16th-century England we would find ourselves in a land very different from how it is today. Ninety per cent of the population lived in villages of 500 people or fewer—an economic unit based on the land. Each year was dominated by the rhythm of ploughing, planting, and harvesting, the villagers working as tenant farmers for the aristocracy or the Church.

Life was short and considered merely an interlude before the life to come, a perspective reinforced by the ever-present, vivid reality of death—tuberculosis, pneumonia, typhoid, and leprosy were widespread; childbirth a deadly hazard for mother and baby.[1] Villagers were largely left to their own medical devices—the very sick usually had to resort to a pilgrimage to Canterbury or some other shrine in the hope of a cure. The bubonic plague (the Black Death) recurrently swept across Europe; in the 14th century it depleted the population of England by at least a third. So many died without access to clergy for the last rites—that essential last sacrament—that the pope had to grant remission of sins to all who succumbed to the dreaded disease.

These successive depopulations deprived the nation of the essential critical mass of people to sustain economic growth. Rather than the rural idyll of plenty that might be imagined it was a cycle of scarcity. In the towns the deprivation was more obvious and mortality rates often higher. London in 1520 was a sprawling slum with a population of 60,000; stinking rubbish and waste of all kinds polluted the streets—lice, fleas, and rats, were commonplace.

Religious and secular life were intermingled in a way unfamiliar in the secular West today. All citizens were subject to Church as well as state law and were required to attend church on Sunday and holy days. Non-compliance might mean an appearance before a Church court which enforced many laws including matters to do with marriage, settling of wills, slander, sexual impropriety, and so on. There was an obligatory tax paid to the Church—the tithe.

To ensure people revered the Church and all it stood for, the terrible future awaiting any who had fallen foul of its sacramental system was everywhere depicted in paintings of suffering souls in hell. There was often a mural over the chancel arch of a church, showing Christ sitting in judgement over naked sinners tumbling out of open graves into the mouths of beasts or the claws of demons. Crosses and statues of saints intended to protect people from evil proliferated in churches. Not only were people reminded of the life to come in these images, pictures, and sermons, but everywhere people went there were religious symbols: at parish boundaries, street crossings, and on bridges.

The whole year in the mainly agricultural economy was structured around the Church calendar—not just Christmas, Lent, Easter, and Whitsuntide, but innumerable saints' days as well. At Rogationtide parishioners marched round the boundaries of their parish beating the ground with sticks to drive out the evil spirits. The devil was considered in a very real sense to be ever present, waiting to waylay the unwary; a subject of humour and caricature today, the devil then was considered a frightening reality and was vividly portrayed in pictures and carvings.[2]

But it was a corrupt Church. The stories told of monastic life in the Middle Ages would make even some of the inured readers of today's popular Sunday papers raise an eyebrow, with priests and nuns often having multiple partners and many illegitimate children, apart from accounts of other unnatural sexual practices. But it must be said in mitigation that these horrors have lost nothing in the telling, and some monasteries escaped them altogether.

The clergy were often illiterate and were supposed to be celibate—but as was pointed out in the 13th century, 'almost none observed it'.[3] It was the practice of the Church to award an office (for example a bishopric) for the benefit of the recipient, not for the benefit of the congregation. On Anne Boleyn's return from France as a young woman, Cardinal Wolsey[4] was the Pope's representative in England and one of the most senior churchmen in the country. He made his illegitimate son Thomas Wynter, while still a schoolboy, dean of Wells, provost of Beverley, archdeacon of York, archdeacon of Richmond, chancellor of Salisbury, prebendary of Wells, York, Salisbury, Lincoln, and Southwell, rector of Rudby in Yorkshire, and St Matthew's, Ipswich. Wolsey himself was a noticeable absentee cleric who amassed a personal fortune from the income accrued.

It was difficult even for the educated to draw a line between superstition and religion in the teachings of the Church. If a baby was baptized accidentally in the name of the Son, Father, and Holy Ghost, rather than Father, Son, and Holy Ghost, the sacrament was considered invalid—and if not corrected it was assumed the child would go to hell. There was not a biblical view of providence, so the most mundane things were often seen as miraculous—a hen laying more eggs than usual might be attributed to the intervention of a saint. An example of a widely held belief was that those who looked on the consecrated bread of the Mass would prosper, and avoid blindness or sudden death, all day. This sort of thinking was not confined to the ignorant—Henry VII ordered 10,000 Masses to be said for his own soul, paying sixpence for each, more than one and a half times the going rate.

It is no surprise to learn that, when the Church and the clergy set such a low moral standard, the general population followed the same path. These were certainly not the 'good old days'—Dickens points out that there was 'a rampant greed and gangsterism ... [that] seem in the legal records to dwarf even the social maladies of our own day.'5

Some might think that this is just the way things were; change was inevitable. But why was England in such a parlous state at this stage of the nation's history? C. S. Lewis memorably said that a nation's culture is the dress of its religion—in other words, the way in which a society conducts itself, its institutions, value systems, and family and national life, is rooted in what it believes.

A Church that believed it had exclusive access to heaven was always an institution susceptible to corruption; the sacramental system caused many to abdicate personal responsibility for their actions, relying instead on the Church to dispense grace by means of one of its sacraments, awarding a penance, or an indulgence; but perhaps most importantly, even if intangibly, the Church's teaching encouraged a worldview that all was fixed: 'ordinary' men and women had no part in the great scheme of things; it was all controlled by the Church.

It was a worldview that was about to be dramatically challenged.

Notes

1 Even if you survived infancy you would not expect to achieve more than forty-five years of age. **Gies,** p. 121.

2 Although the New Testament does warn the unwary of the danger of the devil in 1 Peter 5:8, the mindset of ordinary people at this time, and one that was certainly encouraged by the Church, was such that they imagined he could be scared away with sticks.

3 **Gies,** p. 161.

4 See Appendix 4: Biographical sketches.

5 **Dickens,** p. 38.

Part 2

Anne Boleyn

The early years

Anne Boleyn was born into that medieval world in 1501, not at the Boleyn family home, Hever Castle, but in Norfolk.[1] The second daughter of an aristocratic family, her father was Thomas Boleyn, her grandfather Sir William Boleyn; but more importantly her mother, Elizabeth, was the daughter of Thomas Howard. The Howards were a wealthy and powerful family; Thomas was the second Duke of Norfolk, a title he would pass to his son Thomas—Anne's uncle.

These were the days before meaningful parliamentary democracy, and the Tudor court was where all the power lay. The key factor was being close to the monarch—all the secular authority of the nation ultimately was with him personally; anybody's political career was made or broken on his or her relationship to the monarch. Anne's father was already climbing the political and social hierarchy in his own right and by 1509 he was an important figure at court. Thomas Boleyn has been described as an evangelical. Certainly he was involved in bringing banned evangelical books into England and was considered knowledgeable in the Scriptures—Erasmus, the famous humanist scholar, dedicated a commentary on Psalm 23 to him, calling him 'outstandingly learned'.

It might well be asked how he could be successful at the Tudor court where straight talking, openness, and honesty were not the traits that would gain you advancement. But the court was the world Thomas Boleyn knew, and was the place where careers and fortunes were to be made. He certainly thrived in that environment—he was the best French-speaker at court and had mastered Latin as well. He was a favourite of Henry's at the various war games that Henry loved, including jousting—an event that involved two men in full armour on horseback, racing towards each other while holding out a lance, with the sole aim of dismounting the other rider. Anne's mother was also at court, probably in the service of Catherine of Aragon, Henry's wife,[2] although it is thought some time was spent by her running the household at Hever Castle. Set in the Kent countryside, here there was a home farm, woods, and tenant farms belonging to the estate.[3]

She would no doubt have looked to train her daughters in the skills they would expect to have as married women managing a household. Their son George, Anne's younger brother, would receive a more formal education at Oxford University in readiness for a public career—following in his father's footsteps.

Mary was the Boleyns' eldest child, but Thomas was ambitious for his second daughter, Anne, whom he considered the brighter of the two, so he arranged for her to go abroad for her education. On a previous diplomatic trip he had met the Archduchess Margaret of Austria and had exchanged a friendly bet on the outcome of diplomatic negotiations; Thomas won. He now called in his 'debt' by persuading Margaret to take Anne into her household to train as a maid of honour. Thomas had chosen well, for Margaret was multilingual, an accomplished poet, a patron of the arts, and despite three marriages remained childless, giving her the time to mentor the young Anne. So it was that at the age of twelve Anne began her great adventure—a trip down to the Channel port of Dover, the potentially dangerous sea crossing, then on by road, eventually arriving at Mechelen.[4] It was here that Margaret held court and ruled the Low Countries[5] on behalf of her thirteen-year-old nephew Charles Habsburg, who would become the future Charles V and Holy Roman Emperor.[6] The Habsburg court was a sophisticated and cultured place which would have made an impression on any visitor, let alone a twelve-year-old. Margaret was immediately impressed by the young Anne, writing back to Thomas: 'I find her so bright and pleasant for her young age that I am more beholden to you for sending her to me than you are to me.'[7]

What Anne felt about all this is not known. It was probably her first time away from home and she was alone in a foreign land. But Anne got on with her new life and was put to study under Margaret's tutor. Her first independent letter home to her father, written the following year, is extant today in the library of Corpus Christi College, Cambridge.

She tells of her desire to be a 'woman of good reputation' when she arrives back home—and to be able to speak French well. Another of Anne's tasks was to learn to be a 'lady at court'. This was a serious business. The elaborate dances that played such a part of court life had to be learned and acting skills acquired to enable participation in the various 'masques' (stage performances where the actors often wore masks). The ability to sing and to play a musical instrument were valued attributes. A composite entertainment had been developed with drama, music, and dance brought together round the theme of courtly love, imprisoned maidens, mythical beasts, noble knights, exotic foreigners, wild men, ships in full sail—and more besides. Members of the Habsburg court under Margaret at Mechelen were leaders in the field— far ahead of those at the Tudor court, whom they saw as provincial neighbours.

The whole business of court etiquette had to be mastered: a quick wit and repartee were prized and the correct manner of courtly 'flirtation' was also developed to an art form. The Archduchess was however a strict and meticulous chaperone—everything was to be done 'properly', and according to the 'rules'. Anne was considered a brilliant pupil.

Anne had access to Margaret's extensive collection of books and came into contact with composers and artists—she heard the works of the famous contemporary composer Josquin des Prez, and she probably met Leonardo da Vinci. At this time Anne had the opportunity, unwittingly, to see others who would impact her later life, including Margaret's nephew, the future Emperor Charles V, and, possibly, her own future husband, Henry VIII. The Archduchess, with her court, met Henry when he was negotiating with Emperor Maximilian (Margaret's father) a joint Anglo–imperial attack on France. Henry was an impressive figure at twenty-three: over six feet tall, energetic, athletic, and musically accomplished.[8] He would certainly have put the fourteen-year-old Charles, not an especially handsome boy, in the shade. One can only wonder what Anne's thoughts might have been.

Anne's time at the Mechelen court proved to be short. Despite Henry's negotiations with the Habsburgs, within weeks there was a political U-turn, so common at the time; now an alliance with France was sought. Consequently Mary Tudor, Henry's eighteen-year-old sister, was to be married off (reluctantly) to the decrepit fifty-two-year-old king of France, Louis XII. Thomas Boleyn wrote to Margaret asking her to release Anne, to enable her to be an attendant of Mary Tudor at the wedding. Margaret was reluctant to see her protégée used to smooth the new alliance between England and France, but nonetheless Anne was soon on her way. She travelled by road to Paris and met with her father and older sister Mary— the wedding was to be the occasion of the first family gathering for some years.

But Mary Tudor, the reluctant bride, was soon a widow—Louis XII survived his marriage to her just eighty-two days: he died on 1 January 1515. Claude, Louis XII's daughter, being female, could not inherit the throne. However, the previous year she had married Francis who was next in line to Louis XII; so he became Francis I and she became the new queen—at the age of just fifteen.

Both Anne and her sister Mary had stayed on after Mary Tudor's wedding and witnessed these events. This had been Mary Boleyn's first trip abroad; it would be only natural if she was somewhat jealous of her younger sister and the new sophistication and maturity Anne displayed. Mary determined to experience some of this new world for herself—but rather than the more esoteric skills and pleasures of reading, learning the language, and mastering various musical instruments, Mary opted for the new King Francis's bed. He was a notorious womanizer and Mary Boleyn became one of his mistresses. He soon tired of her and later remarked to an Italian diplomat that she was 'a very great whore, the most infamous of all'.[9]

The contrast between the sisters could not have been greater. Despite all the invective heaped on Anne's memory over the subsequent years, we will see that nobody has ever been able credibly to charge her with being anything but sexually chaste, and a virgin, when she finally consummated her relationship with Henry at the age of thirty-one. Career choices were limited for women in Tudor England. The traditional role was as wife and mother—or, unfortunately, as a mistress, the path Mary Boleyn had chosen. With the rise of the 'new learning' and the Bible in the vernacular, women had access to God's Word for themselves, not through the filter of the male-dominated Church; they now found a new outlet for their energy and intellect. Women like Marguerite d'Angoulême, who was to become a mentor for Anne, became role models for many. Indeed, later in the 16th century fifty-six women were burned at the stake by Queen Mary, Henry's daughter by Catherine of Aragon, for their activities in promoting biblical Christianity.

We can only think that Thomas Boleyn would have disapproved of Mary's behaviour and he did eventually recall her to England, where, however, she promptly became a mistress to Henry VIII. She married William Carey in February 1520—possibly at Henry's behest to disguise the paternity of any children she might have with him. Henry already had one illegitimate child by Elizabeth (Bessie) Blount—Henry Fitzroy—and certainly did not want the claim to his throne muddying any further. But Henry's liaison with Mary was no secret—he named one of his warships after her. This relationship would prove to be a potential problem later when he wanted to marry Anne. As we shall see, he thought he might be tripped up by the affinity rules of Leviticus 18—specifically verse 18: 'Do not take your wife's sister as a rival wife and have sexual relations with her while your wife is living.'

Meanwhile it appears that Anne entered the service of the new Queen Claude. How this happened is not known—perhaps Claude took a liking to Anne: the girls were not a dissimilar age, and she probably interpreted for Claude at the wedding of Louis XII. In any case Anne stayed with Claude in France for nearly seven years, Claude becoming pregnant virtually every year.[10] She died at the age of just twenty-four in 1524.

Court life in Paris was unlikely to have been very different from that in Mechelen. Anne's great skill in singing, dancing, and playing musical instruments was commented on by those who knew her—even those who, at the time they wrote about her abilities, were hostile to her. De Carles, the Spaniard who acted as secretary to the French ambassador at the Tudor court, said: 'La Boullant, who at an early age had come to court, listened carefully to honourable ladies, setting herself to bend all her endeavour to imitate them to perfection, and made such good use of her wits that in no time at all she had command of the language ...'[11]

It is almost certain that Anne would have been present with Claude at the famous Field of the Cloth of Gold, where Henry VIII and Francis I (Claude's husband) met outside Paris in June 1520—so Anne at nineteen may have seen her future husband for a second time. Anne's father had been responsible for all the arrangements, and he had done a magnificent job. The summit was called in the name of peace and friendship, but became an event for each nation to outdo the other in displays of wealth and power; the tents and the costumes displayed so much 'cloth of gold' (an expensive fabric woven with silk and gold thread) that the site of the meeting was named after it. Also present, it seems, were Anne's younger brother George and her sister Mary.

It was during Anne's years at the French court that she came into contact with Marguerite d'Angoulême (Duchess of Alençon, later Queen of Navarre), ten years Anne's senior and sister to the French King Francis I. Marguerite was influenced by the Reformers Luther, Calvin, and Jacques Lefèvre d'Étaples. The last of these had spoken out openly against the Roman Catholic Church five years before Luther emerged onto the scene. His commentary on Paul's letters, which Anne read, had been published in France in 1512.

It is remarkable that Marguerite, in the midst of the French court, openly promoted her faith and supported evangelical efforts. She provided the high-level political patronage that protected Reformers from the Faculty of Theology (known as the Sorbonne) in Paris. Some writers have commented that Marguerite never officially renounced her Catholicism, but we must be careful to realize the nature of the times. How do we define an evangelical? There were no great Reformed credal statements. Biblical doctrine was emerging piecemeal from the obfuscating fog of the Roman Catholic Church at that time. Settled convictions took several years to formulate. Marguerite—and, as shall be seen, Anne herself—never left some Catholic doctrines behind. But Marguerite surely was an evangelical. Why? Because she saw that the Bible was God's word and she loved the doctrine of justification by faith. Furthermore, in the way in which she tried to protect those of similar persuasion from her own brother's persecutions, she showed that she was no armchair theologian speculating on the nature of religion. Marguerite twice had to intervene for Louis de Berquin (a translator of both Erasmus and Luther) to stop him being killed as a heretic, and in 1521 Lefèvre had to be rescued from a lynch mob at the Sorbonne.

She wrote of her own experience:

I have found only one true and perfect remedy, which is reading the Holy Scriptures. In perusing them, my mind experiences its true and perfect joy; and from this pleasure of the mind, proceeds the repose and health of the body … I take up the Psalms and sing them with my heart and pronounce with my tongue, as humbly as possible, the fine hymns with which the Holy Spirit inspired David and the sacred authors.[12]

Little is known of this time in Anne's life—but it is certain that she established a close friendship with Marguerite. It also seems clear that Anne came to know for herself that same joy Marguerite had, probably some time during her stay at the French court; she saw for herself that faith was placed in the heart by the Holy Spirit. For a thousand years Europe had been taught that the Christian religion was about submitting to a ritualistic system, a system that had no basis in the Bible. Now Anne realized that no amount of penance could atone for sin; forgiveness was entirely God's gift and the appropriate response for a believer was heartfelt joy and thankfulness. It was a life-changing experience for Anne—as it is for all those who receive it. It was to sustain her through some heady, triumphant, and tragic times that, unknown to her, lay ahead.

All Anne's early contact with Reformed teaching came through French literature, French being one of the foremost languages of the 'new learning'. She owned several works by Lefèvre, in later life treasuring a 1534 edition of the Bible in French translated by him. Its covers were inscribed with 'As in Adam all die, so will all be raised in Christ', a summary of Romans 5:12–18 and John 1:17: 'For the law was given through Moses; grace and truth came through Jesus Christ.' These were—and are—core evangelical teachings. Other works she owned included an evangelical commentary on Ecclesiastes, and a copy of Le Pasteur Évangélique (The Gospel Shepherd) by Clément Marot.

Later in life Anne wrote to Marguerite saying 'that her greatest wish, next to having a son, was to see you again.'[13] This could in part be what we would consider the excessive courtesies of the day—but two years previously the Duke of Norfolk, after extensive consultations with Marguerite, had written to Henry that Marguerite was 'as affectionate to your highness as if she were your own sister, and likewise to the queen [Anne].'[14]

Further, in July 1534, Henry had a meeting arranged with Francis I which for domestic political reasons he wanted to avoid, so he got Anne to write to Marguerite (sister of Francis) to postpone it until the following year. Anne wrote and told her that she was expecting a child and so did not want to travel. All this suggests a very close relationship indeed between the two women—so close it could be used as a lever to smooth over Henry's awkward relationship with France. It is difficult not to see that this friendship was born of the fact that Anne's personal faith in Christ, and her understanding of the gospel, dated from her time with Marguerite.[15]

So what happened to the French Reformation? Marguerite d'Angoulême did not have sufficient influence or power—or, some would say, a sufficiently clear grasp of the gospel—to facilitate the reforms. Moreover, while Cambridge University in England became a seedbed for new ideas and fostered the 'new learning', the Sorbonne in Paris stood against change. Nearly all those who embraced the biblical gospel in France were not people of influence—Marguerite was a notable exception. In October 1534 several cities in France woke to find their walls plastered with notices placed there by many ordinary French men and women. They denounced in strong language the Catholic doctrine of the Mass. There was a swift and bloody response from Francis I, who said, 'Let all be seized and let Lutheranism be totally exterminated'. A reign of terror ensued; even Marguerite, Francis I's own sister, was threatened. She fled to the Pyrenees with many fellow-believers. The year 1534 marked the end of Lutheran success in France and any hope that the Reformation might gain a foothold there.

Elton comments that Reformation in Europe required influential secular support to carry through radical change in a nation.[16] History does seem to agree with this conclusion. Even though in England Wycliffe had translated the Bible into English more than a hundred years before, access to it was very limited. It had been written in an English that was old-fashioned even for its own time and was a translation from the Latin text—not from the original Hebrew and Greek that Tyndale and others would use. But more importantly than this, the Roman Catholic Church had dominated English daily life and its institutions for centuries; there were powerful vested interests in maintaining the status quo. The Church strongly discouraged Bible reading by lay people and prosecuted those involved in translating or distributing any Bible translations or evangelical books.

But God had determined that England's destiny was to be different from that of its European neighbour, and to achieve that he had chosen a young, slight, intelligent woman to play a pivotal part. Anne was in the only place in the world that humanly speaking could have equipped her to achieve the outcome that was required: to gain the courtly skills that would 'wow' the establishment in England; to find the mentors who would not only lead her to Christ, but also serve as role models of how to survive in such an unbelieving court; and to have access to the Reformed literature that would give her a clear enough grasp of the gospel to withstand the pressure that was to come. It was all there at the sophisticated, worldly, unbelieving, unknowing French court. God was preparing Anne for her life's work. The Bible is clear: 'In him we were also chosen, having been predestined according to the plan of him who works out everything in conformity with the purpose of his will.'[17]

At the age of twenty Anne was ready for her destiny, and late in 1521 she was abruptly summoned back to England. A relation of Anne's in Ireland, Thomas Butler, Earl of Ormonde, had died in 1515 leaving the Boleyns and the St Legers as joint heirs-general. But there was a dispute—another relative, Piers Butler, who lived in Ireland, was not giving up his claim, styling himself Earl of Ormonde. Piers had a son, James, and it was suggested, perhaps by Anne's Uncle Thomas, that Anne should marry James, bringing the lands and title back into the family. It seemed an elegant solution. The fact that Anne was probably not consulted was not unusual. Aristocratic families saw the family as a sort of firm: maximum effort was put in to advance family interests and secure its position, not just for the present, but for future generations as well. This was done by currying favour with the monarch to gain land and titles—and by marrying any sons or daughters off in an advantageous match.

But this match was not to be. As we shall see, when Anne arrived in England the quasi-engagement dragged on and Anne eventually had other suitors—among them the King of England.

Chapter 3

Notes

1 The place and date of her birth have been in dispute, but Ives and others are confident of both. See **Ives,** *The Life and Death of Anne Boleyn,* p. 3.

2 See Appendix 4: Biographical sketches.

3 Hever Castle today contains visitor attractions, information, and displays about its history, including its most famous occupant, Anne Boleyn.

4 In modern-day Belgium. Much of Margaret's palace still stands today.

5 A large area of northern Europe embracing, but not exactly corresponding to, the present-day Netherlands, Belgium, and Luxembourg.

6 Holy Roman Emperor was the title given to the ruler of the area of land which today forms central Europe. One of the tasks of the emperor was to protect the Roman Catholic Church, the pope duly crowning him—hence the title 'Emperor'. An elected role rather than strictly hereditary, it was nonetheless held by the Habsburg family for many years. The Holy Roman Empire lasted until 1806.

7 **Denny,** p. 29.

8 Henry VIII might have been the composer of the famous English song *Greensleeves*—possibly written for Anne Boleyn. See **Denny,** p. 54.

9 **Denny,** p. 38.

10 **Starkey** in *The Reign of Henry VIII* has Anne in England for at least some of this time—see p. 74. However **Ives,** *The Life and Death of Anne Boleyn* (his more recently published work) sees Anne as being in France the whole time—see pp. 29–31.

11 **Denny,** pp. 27–28.

12 Quoted in **Denny,** p. 94.

13 **Ives,** *The Life and Death of Anne Boleyn*, p. 33.

14 Ibid.

15 It is known that others at the French court were interested in the 'new learning', including Queen Claude. Although Anne's contact with Marguerite might have been limited, it is she who had the clear testimony of personal faith in Christ. See **Ives,** *The Life and Death of Anne Boleyn*, p. 278.

16 See **Elton,** pp. 35ff.

17 Ephesians 1:11.

Anne at the Tudor court

Anne started her long journey home. Met by her father at Calais, they undertook the hazardous crossing to Dover, and then went on to London, perhaps stopping at the family home Hever Castle on the way. Many historians choose 1520 to mark the end of the Middle Ages and the beginning of the modern era. Father and daughter would have had no concept of this as they rode on horseback along the rutted and muddy roads of Kent that December of 1521—nor that they were going to be involved in one of the great dramas of English history. And not just as bystanders: Anne would herself be responsible for many of the tumultuous events that changed the nation's history for ever, her new-found faith leading her to an early death—the first Queen of England to be executed.

They arrived safely in London and Thomas was, no doubt, proud to show off his daughter, newly arrived from France. Her first court appearance was at the lavish twelve-day Christmas celebrations. The focus of much attention, Anne would have been asked many questions about the latest gossip and fashions at the French court as Thomas introduced her to his friends—including the King. It was when presents were exchanged at New Year that Anne wore the stylish yellow gown that caused so much comment. The contemporary Spaniard Lancelot de Carles said, 'No one would ever have taken her to be English by her manners, but a native-born Frenchwoman.'[1]

Anne became a lady-in-waiting for Queen Catherine. Her duties were that of a professional entertainer—making elegant conversation, singing, playing musical instruments, and taking part in masques and dancing. She would have been completely at home in her new surroundings—her time in the Habsburg and French courts had prepared her well.

In March 1522 there were to be celebrations at the English court to mark the decision by Henry to ally himself with Charles (King of Spain and in line to become the next Holy Roman Emperor) rather than with Francis I (King of France, husband to Queen Claude)—yet another U-turn in foreign policy. Charles was to visit England and be betrothed to Henry's daughter by Catherine of Aragon, Princess Mary (another marriage that was never to be). The celebrations were to be suitably extravagant to impress the future Emperor—a masque in the style that the Habsburg court had made famous to be held at Cardinal Wolsey's palace, York Place (later Whitehall Palace), on 4 March— Shrove Tuesday, the last day before Lent, known today as Pancake Day.

Every masque had a theme; this one was to be the cruelty of unrequited love, and the climax was an assault on a mock castle. There were eight masked court ladies, each representing an aspect of love, and eight men, each representing an aspect of chivalric tradition. The ladies were in the castle, protected from assault by eight choristers manning the lower walls.

Anne was selected to play Perseverance, the other seven parts all being played by important women at court, including Henry's sister Mary as Beauty. Promoted straight into this premier league, Anne dazzled others with her sense of dress, her natural style, and her skill in acting and singing. She had obviously made a big impression in a short time; she was back in England doing what she had learnt to do so well while abroad.

The men approached and begged the ladies to come down; they refused, then, to a peal of cannon, the castle was bombarded, Henry VIII dressed as Ardent Desire. Although most are probably familiar with Henry's portraits in later life which show his physical decline, at this time he was still only thirty and an impressive figure; tall, with an athletic frame, clean-shaven, with piercing blue eyes. His clothes were of gold or silver, his fingers full of jewels, and around his neck was a gold collar from which hung a huge diamond. With the background noise of live cannon shots he led the attack—dates, oranges, and other fruits serving as ammunition. The ladies of course succumbed, dancing ensued, the masks came off, and the banquet began.

Henry as Ardent Desire and Anne as Perseverance—with hindsight they proved to be remarkably apt roles, ones they would play out in their relationship over the next decade and more.

What of Anne's physical appearance at this time? Later accounts of what she actually looked like are often heavily influenced by the religious persuasion of the person giving the account—some keen to portray her as an evil woman with physical deformities to match; most of these can be dismissed. However, many have said that she had a sixth finger, or at least the malformation of a finger tip. Denny, in her recent biography, thinks that even this is unlikely—and given that Henry's superstitions were those of the day (linking deformity with witchcraft) the balance of evidence is surely against it.[2] Even allowing for this it does not seem that Anne was a conventional beauty; the Venetian diplomat thought: 'Not one of the handsomest women in the world; she is of middling stature, swarthy complexion [the fashion was to be pale], long neck, wide mouth, a bosom not much raised ['bosoms' were 'in'—and it seems Anne was not especially well endowed] and eyes which are black and beautiful.'[3]

Several commented on her eyes, which were probably hazel brown—de Carles wrote that they were '... always most attractive which she knew well how to use with effect. Sometimes leaving them at rest and at others, sending a message to carry the secret witness of the heart. And, truth to tell, such was their power that many surrendered to their obedience.'[4]

Her hair, which she wore long, was probably a rich auburn colour rather than dark as some suggest—certainly not the fashionable blonde. It was obviously a striking feature, one remarked on by those who saw her. Anne's mother Elizabeth Howard was considered to be a very great beauty, so Anne's distinctive looks might have come from her, and the reddish tinge to her hair perhaps from her Irish ancestry. What is certain is that Anne was more than the sum of her parts. She was always careful to dress well and 'every day made some change in the fashion of her garments.'[5] She exuded style and charisma. In an age where everything French was fashionable, where everybody wanted to have that sophisticated French gloss, after seven years in the court of the French queen, Anne had what it took. Starkey says: '... Anne came back to [the Tudor] court that might have been designed as the perfect stage for her talents. Everybody was trying to be French; she was French.'[6]

It seems that no contemporary portrait of Anne has survived—the drawings by Holbein that some say are of Anne are unlikely to be authentic. This absence could be explained by the backlash against Anne in the years after her death—both against her personally and against the religious reforms in which she played such an important part. But we can be sure that the enamelled portrait in the ring that Queen Elizabeth I (Anne's daughter) wore is a good likeness—many close to Elizabeth knew her mother. This image is similar to the portrait medal of 1534 to be found in the British Museum, and the portrait by an anonymous painter at Hever Castle showing Anne holding a single rose. If the painting in Britain's Royal Collection by an anonymous painter of Princess Elizabeth aged thirteen is a good likeness of her, the future queen bore a striking similarity to her mother.

The portrait at Hever shows Anne in a black gown and wearing the French hood she was known for. This jewelled headdress set on the back of the head showing her hair was a remarkable departure in fashion—for 300 years women had kept their hair covered. Some considered this an adventurous, even shocking style—perhaps because of what Paul teaches in the New Testament where he seems to say that a woman's hair should be covered.7 The fashion for the French hood lapsed on Anne's death but interestingly her daughter often wore a similar one, perhaps in homage to her mother.

What is the 21st-century Christian to make of all this, especially in light of the following teaching from the Bible in 1 Timothy 2:9? 'I also want women to dress modestly, with decency and propriety, not with braided hair or gold or pearls or expensive clothes, but with good deeds, appropriate for women who profess to worship God.'

Isn't the apostle Paul saying that a woman's beauty is not defined by these things, rather than necessarily forbidding them? Except for showing more of her hair than was customary at the time, there is no suggestion that Anne did not dress with decency or propriety—but she certainly loved fine clothes and expensive jewellery. In this respect perhaps a comparison could be made in our own generation with the late Diana, Princess of Wales. She knew how to dress stylishly and it became part of her image—it was expected of her by the public and her peers. When Anne became queen everybody similarly expected her to dress the part—and she did.

It was not long before Henry Percy, a young man in Cardinal Wolsey's household and heir to the earldom of Northumberland, fell for Anne—totally. But sadly for him the match was not to be; some have said that the King warned Wolsey to keep Henry Percy away from Anne because of his own interest in her, but at this early stage it is unlikely. More probably the problem lay with Anne's 'engagement' to James Butler—the reason for her return from France. Henry Percy was distraught on being told and burst into tears—his feelings for Anne went very deep. He claimed the right to choose his own bride, not the match his father had chosen. But there was no arguing with his father, or Cardinal Wolsey. His eventual marriage to Mary Talbot did not last; his physical and mental health declined and he died young.

What were Anne's real feelings for Henry Percy? Had Anne in any way encouraged him? It is not known. Could this relationship have led to the failure of the Boleyn–Butler marriage plan? It is possible. To understand why, it is necessary to understand the nature of a marriage contract in 16th-century England. If a couple promised themselves to each other it could be considered a binding marriage contract. If they consummated the relationship sexually it certainly would be—and any official ceremony that was to be held would follow; this would not be considered in any way immoral. In other words, the commitment and the act were the marriage—there was not the same emphasis we have today on a ceremony. All this was governed by canon (that is Church) law, not statute law; there was no separate legal, formal, registration of marriages as exists in the UK today. Were Henry Percy and Anne 'married'? Probably not—and certainly there was no sexual consummation—but the nature of Anne's relationship with Henry Percy will figure later in the story. During all this Anne's father was abroad on diplomatic business. When he returned, alarmed at the prospect of his marriage plans for her falling apart, he withdrew Anne from court back to the family home at Hever.

There is no evidence to support the suggestion made by some that Anne never forgave Cardinal Wolsey for the break in her relationship with Henry Percy. The relationship between the Boleyns and Wolsey always contained within it the possibility of discord. The Cardinal represented the old Catholic religion and much that was wrong with it. The Boleyns, as evangelicals, were in favour of reform of the Church. Wolsey was a powerful figure who stood for the status quo. He was already a member of the Privy Council when he was made a cardinal in the Church, and in the same year he was appointed Lord Chancellor by Henry—the post usually went to a cleric—demonstrating the 16th-century fusion of Church and State that the modern mind might find difficult to grasp.

Henry Percy was not Anne's only suitor. Henry VIII loved to play the

Renaissance man: an intellectual, a sponsor of the arts. His own abilities have perhaps been exaggerated by contemporary accounts—there was nothing lost in flattering a powerful monarch; certainly the praise heaped on him by Erasmus needs to be treated circumspectly. But music and the arts were an important part of life at court and Henry had gathered there some of Europe's most famous musicians.

Anne's abilities attracted a band of admirers: '… when she sang, like a second Orpheus, she would have made bears and wolves attentive.'[8] This was too much for one of the most famous poets of the day, Thomas Wyatt. Although a (separated) married man he too fell for Anne. It is almost certain that some of his poetry was inspired by Anne and his feelings for her.[9] But it is difficult to assess how much in his poetry is autobiographical, and how much is down to the game of courtly love that most at court enjoyed playing. Certainly Wyatt was in love with Anne—as, it seems, were others. We know of Wyatt's feelings because in coded language they can be found in his work. But poetry is poetry, expressing the emotional world of the writer; his feelings might not have been reciprocated. Despite some later Catholic sources saying differently, there is no evidence whatsoever that they had an 'affair', and again it is certain that there was no consummation of the relationship. Some years later, in 1530, when Anne was being courted by Henry VIII, there was comment by the Duke of Suffolk (Mary Tudor's new husband Charles Brandon) on the relationship. Anne insisted Wyatt be sent from court, something Henry was reluctant to do—a reluctance that belies any suspicion of the allegations that had been made. Suffolk was merely attempting to derail what he saw as a potentially disastrous alliance for him—that between the King and the Boleyns.

George Cavendish, a Catholic writer antagonistic to Anne, was an eyewitness of the events at this time, and surely outlined the truth when in his Metrical Visions he saw Anne as a virgin on her marriage to Henry, and had her say:

The noblest prince that reigned on the ground
I had to my husband. He took me to his wife;
At home with my father a maiden he me found.[10]

Notes

1 Quoted by **Denny,** p. 5.

2 **Denny,** pp. 16–17.

3 Quoted by **Ives,** *The Life and Death of Anne Boleyn,* p. 40.

4 Quoted by **Denny,** p. 20.

5 Quoted by **Ives,** *The Life and Death of Anne Boleyn*, p. 45.

6 **Starkey,** *The Reign of Henry VIII,* p. 75.

7 1 Corinthians 11:3–16—although the NIV makes the passage read so that the covering Paul refers to is the hair itself, to my mind the best interpretation.

8 See **Denny,** p. 53.

9 For example, '*If waker care, if sudden pale colour*'.

10 Quoted by **Denny,** p. 108.

A king in love

It was now 1526; Anne was twenty-five and had been back in England some four years—and with each year her marriage prospects declined. The proposed match with James Butler had fallen through, and although she had plenty of suitors none, it seemed, had been considered a suitable match to progress the 'family firm'—or perhaps none had offered marriage. Anne was a noticeably opinionated and independent young woman and this would not have gone down well with some. But it did with the King. When he first took a romantic interest in Anne is not known, but there is an account of a bowls match he had with Thomas Wyatt where he revealed his feelings for her. Wyatt had 'stolen' an item of jewellery from Anne and wore it round his neck, teasing Anne about it and suggesting that she claim it back; it was all part of the flirtations of court dalliance. Similarly the King had taken from her a ring and wore it on his little finger.

Ives tells the story, quoting from an account by George Wyatt (grandson of Thomas):

Playing bowls with Thomas and some other courtiers, Henry claimed that his wood held shot when it clearly did not; pointing with his little finger with the ring on it, 'he said, "Wyatt, I tell thee it is mine", smiling upon him withal.' The point was taken, but Wyatt, 'pausing a little, and finding the king bent to pleasure', decided on a bold response. He produced Anne's jewel and proceeded to use the ribbon to measure the distances, remarking, 'If it may like your majesty to give me leave to measure it, I hope it will be mine.' The king's good humour vanished—'It may be so, but then am I deceived'—and he stalked off to see Anne. She, discovering what was wrong, explained the business of the jewel to Henry, and sunlight was restored.[1]

What was the nature of Henry's interest in Anne? He had recently finished his relationship with Mary Boleyn and probably thought that he could start a similar relationship with her sister. Although his marriage to Catherine of Aragon at first appeared to have been a good one with genuine affection on both sides, there had been no sexual relations for the past two years. She was now thirty-nine—nearly six years older than

Henry. Her petite figure was no more, and some considered the ritualistic observance of her religious duties obsessive—she certainly had no time for court frivolities. Anne was a vivacious woman of twenty-five who sparkled at court, Henry's playground. He was smitten.

Thomas Wyatt now knew that he had no chance of winning Anne; Henry had her marked out for himself. In his most famous poem Wyatt refers to this new situation:

Whoso list to hunt, I know where is a hind.
But as for me, alas I may no more:
The vain travail hath wearied me so sore.
I am of them that farthest cometh behinde.
Yet may I by no means my wearied mind
Draw from the deer, but as she fleeth afore
Fainting I follow. I leave off therefore,
Sithens in a net I seek to hold the wind.
Who list to hunt, I put him out of doubt,
As well as I may spend his time in vain,
And graven with diamonds in letters plain
There is written her fair neck round about.
'Noli me tangere, for Caesar's I am,
And wild for to hold, though I seem tame.'[2]

Caesar is Henry, and 'Noli me tangere' is a quote from the Latin Vulgate text of the New Testament where Jesus in his newly resurrected body says to Mary, 'Touch me not'. Wyatt's poetry does not disguise a sinister element in Henry's pursuit of her. Anne is the hind running from the hunter; her fate is to be caught and slain. Perhaps to underline her new position, one of Henry's earliest gifts to her was a buck he had killed in a hunt. He suggested she might enjoy eating it, but the symbolism could not be missed.

There exist in the Vatican library in Rome seventeen letters that Henry wrote to Anne, probably secretly taken from Anne in her lifetime by a representative of the Church in an effort to prove that the real motivation for the King's 'divorce' from Catherine was a sexual relationship with

Anne. But instead they show Anne resisting this most powerful of monarchs as he pleads with her in increasingly desperate terms. Anne's replies have not survived; they were almost certainly destroyed on her death by those wishing to eradicate any memory of her. Unfortunately none of Henry's letters are dated, but from their content an approximate sequence can be deduced. In the first three, writing in his own hand, Henry is trying to woo Anne. Although he uses the language of courtly love, it is clear that he proposes more. In the first (extant) letter, probably sent in 1526 (Anne is most likely away from court at Hever), he complains that she has not replied to an earlier letter; it is obvious from the content of Henry's next letter that Anne has now replied and made clear that she is wary of this new suitor. In the third letter he begins to show the depth of his feeling for Anne, and his confusion at what he sees as mixed signals from her:

Debating with myself the contents of your letter, I have put myself in great distress, not knowing how to interpret them, whether to my disadvantage, as in some places is shown, or to advantage as in others I understand them; praying you with all my heart that you will expressly certify me of your whole mind concerning the love between us two. For of necessity I must ensure me of this answer having been now above one whole year struck with the dart of love, not being assured either of failure or of finding place in your heart and grounded affection. Which last point has kept me for some little time from calling you my mistress, since if you do not love me in a way which is beyond common affection that name in no wise belongs to you, for it denotes a singular love, far removed from the common.

Then going to the point:

If it shall please you to do me the office of a true, loyal mistress and friend and to give yourself up, body and soul, to me who will be and have been your loyal servant (if by your severity you do not forbid me), I promise you that not only shall the name be given you, but that also I will take you for my only mistress, rejecting from thought and affection all others save yourself, to serve you only.3

Henry seems to be suggesting that Anne should have the position of an honoured mistress, 'maîtresse en titre', in the tradition of the French kings.

Anne's response to this particular letter is not recorded, but what is told on another occasion is that Anne:

… fell down upon her knees saying, 'I think your majesty, most noble and worthy king, speaketh these words in mirth to prove me, without intent of defiling your princely self, who I find thinks nothing less than of such wickedness which would justly procure the hatred of God and of your good queen against us … I have already given my maidenhead into my husband's hands.'4

In other words, Anne is saying that her virginity is being saved for her future husband. After a long silence (Anne had again retreated to Hever) Henry writes:

Since I parted with you I have been advised that the opinion in which I left you is now altogether changed and that you will not come to court neither with my lady your mother, and if you could, nor yet by any other way. The which report being true I cannot enough marvel at, seeing that I am well assured I have never since that time committed fault … I could do none other than lament me of my ill fortune, abating by little and little my so great folly.5

Henry thinks Anne is staying away from court deliberately to avoid him, something in his vanity he 'cannot enough marvel at'. And what is more, she is offended by his suggestion that she become his mistress—which Henry now sees as a mistake: a 'great folly'.

What are we to make of all this? Henry was a man used to getting his own way—he never had to plead for anything. But here he was not just pleading but recognizing that he was making mistakes. Henry had a strong dislike of admitting any errors, let alone recording it in a letter—it is known that he hated writing anything. In Henry's position women were not to be wooed, but to be negotiated for by diplomats, or simply commanded into his bed as his mistresses. Starkey describes Anne's behaviour as 'audacious' for the times, submitting Henry to a remarkable humiliation.6 Certainly Anne was not accepting the conventions of the day; she was making a stand.

Why was Henry subjecting himself to this? He truly was struck by the 'dart of love', and was prepared to go to great lengths to win her. He too was throwing convention to the wind, embarking on this letter-writing tack; he acted as a humble supplicant, not the supreme monarch he was, almost begging for Anne to reciprocate with some sign of affection. It will be seen that eventually his love for Anne Boleyn caused him to cast to one side much more than convention. To get the woman he wanted Henry VIII showed that he was prepared to sacrifice everything: his friends, his allies at home and abroad, his religion, even, as some would see it, his own soul, when he was excommunicated by the Church—its ultimate punishment.

And what about Anne? Did she accept Henry as a suitor—and, if so, why? Henry was one of the most powerful and ruthless men in Europe. It can be seen in this early correspondence that she was desperately trying to keep Henry at arm's length. For Anne it must have been like being in a cage with a hungry and restless lion. If she antagonized Henry it would damage not only her but also her family—her father, brother, and uncle, all had important places at court. Her frequent absences from court and her ambiguous replies to Henry, which left him confused, show that far from encouraging him, she was trying to avoid the King without offending him. It is difficult to see how she could have handled things differently in these early years.

But there did come a turning point. Henry realized that to have Anne he would have to offer her marriage. In June 1527 Henry told Catherine he was seeking an annulment of their marriage. Ives, in a detailed analysis, makes it clear that Anne up to this point had firmly resisted Henry's advances.[7] And certainly at this stage no one at court suspected Anne of being in any sort of relationship with Henry. It was now that she sent Henry a small gift—a model of a ship with a woman on board wearing a diamond pendant. In the symbolism of the day a ship meant protection (as in Noah's Ark); the diamond was representative of the heart. Henry knew what it meant—the heart was Anne's, and he was the ship of protection.

Henry was effusive in his letter of reply: 'For so beautiful a gift, and so exceeding (taking it in all), I thank you right cordially; not alone for the fair diamond and the ship in which the solitary damsel is tossed about, but chiefly for the good intent and too-humble submission vouchsafed in this by your kindness …'[8]

Henry was overjoyed. It is clear he had understood the significance of the gift. His phrase 'so exceeding (taking it in all)' makes it plain that he knew Anne was offering herself as a potential wife. And here is the crucial question. Why did Anne send this gift and so signal to Henry that she would accept him as a suitor? He was a married man, and she had rightly resisted his advances for at least two years. What had changed?

There are several possible answers:

- Anne had simply given up the fight. She had been worn down by Henry and feared the consequences of resisting him anymore.
- She had become attracted to him. He was undoubtedly an impressive figure—tall, good looking (at least at this stage), and accomplished in many areas including the arts.
- She saw that an annulment was possible and that she could become Henry's legitimate wife and queen, a tremendously powerful position from which she could advance the reform agenda.

All these things might have been factors. To help answer the question, the dating of the above exchange is important—and the subject of much debate. Starkey dates Anne's letter 1 January 1527, which would make Anne's acceptance of Henry as a suitor a catalyst for Henry pursuing the annulment of his marriage with Catherine.[9] Ives argues strongly for a later date—probably July of that same year—that is, after Henry had written to Catherine in the June telling her that he was to seek an annulment.[10]

Based on what is known about Anne's bold and unequivocal stand against Henry so far, the latter is the more probable timetable. Once Henry had made the first tangible moves to annul his marriage and Anne could see herself as queen, she conceded and began to accept his advances.

Most of the books about Anne Boleyn talk about Henry's 'divorce'—but the Roman Catholic Church then, as today, did not accept divorce. Marriage, it taught, was a sacrament. It had been endorsed in heaven and nothing could 'put it asunder', not even the pope himself; there was no divorce.[11] But if it could be shown that the marriage sacrament had in some way not been performed correctly—or that the relationship was invalid—then nothing had happened in heaven: the marriage was not endorsed there and so did not take place, making Henry a single man. And Henry claimed just that. He said that his marriage to Catherine, his brother's widow, was incest (for reasons we shall see in the next chapter), despite the papal dispensation that enabled it to take place.

This might seem a subtle distinction for many today—but those who concurred with Henry about the invalidity of the papal dispensation by definition accepted that Anne was courting, and eventually marrying, a single man. If the validity of the papal dispensation was upheld, she was not. But it does not do Anne Boleyn justice for us to say, with a 500-year retrospective view, that it can be seen that both Henry's arguments, and those of the Church, were false—and that Anne should have acted differently.

Once Henry made a move to have the annulment of his marriage declared, whatever her personal feelings for him were, she saw the possibility that marriage to Henry offered. The Reformation was gathering apace in mainland Europe and penetrating England. Books were being smuggled into the country that threatened the future of the Roman Catholic Church; many involved were risking their lives. Anne was sympathetic to their cause and the 'new learning' the books contained. Surely even at this early stage Anne could see she could play a great part in influencing the King and so furthering the evangelical cause she believed in, and in using that influence to protect believers who were being actively persecuted. She had the clear example of her mentor Marguerite, sister to the unbelieving French king. Did Anne now see that she could be a Queen Esther to Henry? In the Old Testament book Esther, the Jewish heroine of the story marries the unbelieving King Xerxes (called Ahasuerus in some translations) in order to save her people from persecution. Certainly during Anne's reign many saw her as such.

We simply do not know. 1 Corinthians 13, the great chapter in the Bible about love, tells us that love always trusts. Surely it is beholden on Christian believers to trust that Anne Boleyn's motives were good, especially when we look at her record once she became queen. What is certain is that many people in England, who during her reign, and subsequently, came to love the Bible and the Saviour it speaks about, were grateful for her decision to take on the daunting task of becoming consort to the powerful, mercurial, and unpredictable Henry VIII.

Notes

1 **Ives,** *The Life and Death of Anne Boleyn,* p. 82.
2 Quoted by **Denny,** p. 92.
3 **Ives,** *The Life and Death of Anne Boleyn,* p. 85.
4 Ibid.
5 **Denny,** p. 63.
6 **Starkey,** *Six wives: the queens of Henry VIII,* p. 283.
7 **Ives,** *The Life and Death of Anne Boleyn,* pp. 84–90.
8 Ibid. p. 87.
9 Ibid. p. 282.
10 Ibid. pp. 88–91.
11 See **Kreeft,** p. 360.

The King's 'great matter'

Henry's intention to have his marriage to Catherine annulled and to marry Anne was one thing; achieving it was another. For the next six years it dominated his thinking—it became the King's 'great matter'. The obstacles were enormous. They included the ever-dominant Roman Catholic Church, powerful potential, or actual, enemies abroad, huge vested interests in the country, and much popular opinion—as well as the resourceful and tenacious Catherine. Certainly Henry, by his own account, was 'in love'. But that alone is not sufficient to explain his perseverance during the next six years of extended wrangling with the Pope to secure an annulment and gain a legitimate marriage to Anne. Before his long 'engagement' to Anne is considered, it is useful to see the other factors that bore down on Henry.

It was a principal duty of a king to produce a legitimate male heir, and he had not done so. In any kingdom this was critical, but it was especially so for Henry, who always thought his hold on power was tenuous. This perspective is understandable when the background of the Tudor claim to the throne is considered. Richard II was overthrown in 1399 by Henry Bolingbroke of Lancaster—he became Henry IV. Richard II had no sons, but Henry had four, and this undoubtedly was why his dramatic seizure of the crown was so widely accepted. But this did not stop Richard Duke of York pressing his claim to the throne, plunging the country into protracted civil wars—the Wars of the Roses: York versus Lancaster. Henry IV died in 1413 and the throne passed to his son, Henry V. Henry V managed, largely on the battlefield, to unify the crowns of France and England. But he died young and the throne passed to his son who became Henry VI at just nine months old. In the course of his reign he lost most of France and his sanity. He was succeeded by Edward IV, whose twelve-year-old son Edward V inherited the crown on his father's death. His uncle, Richard of Gloucester, was appointed Lord Protector, but he imprisoned Edward and his younger brother in the Tower of London and declared himself Richard III. Some hold that he had his nephews murdered. Although an extremely able king, he had no heir, leaving him vulnerable to rival claimants—notably the Tudors.

The Tudor dynasty arose from an affair between Henry V's young widow, Catherine de Valois, and Owen ap Meredith ap Tudor—a low-born groom with no royal blood in his veins. The eldest son by this relationship, Edmund, married Margaret Beaufort, an illegitimate descendant of the Lancaster family. Their son Henry defeated Richard III at the famous battle of Bosworth in 1485 and seized the crown for himself, becoming Henry VII.

Henry VII helped consolidate his hold on the throne by his marriage in 1486 to Elizabeth of York, daughter of Edward IV. But his own claim to a royal line was still tenuous, and a crown won on the battlefield could always be lost there; throughout his reign there was always someone ready to dispute his hold on it. Elizabeth and Henry had two surviving boys, Arthur born in 1486, and Henry in 1491. In 1497 Henry junior, aged just six, later to be Henry VIII, took refuge in the Tower of London with his mother while his father battled against Perkin Warbeck and his supporters, as they tried to seize the crown back from the Tudors. He never forgot the experience.

Henry VII wanted Catherine of Aragon as the bride for his son Arthur in order to cement an alliance with Spain. The king of Spain doubted the grip the Tudors had on the throne, so refused to give his daughter in marriage while Warbeck (now in the Tower), or the Earl of Warwick, another contender for the throne, were alive. Henry VII had them both executed, the execution witnessed by the appropriate Spanish authorities. The way was now clear for Arthur's marriage on 14 November 1501. He was seventeen and Catherine only sixteen, and within five months she was a widow, Arthur having died—probably of tuberculosis. This meant that Catherine should go back to Spain—with her dowry of 200,000 ducats. Henry VII, keen to keep the alliance with Spain, to say nothing of the 200,000 ducats, suggested she marry Arthur's brother Henry. The eleven-year-old Henry was yet to be married off, so it seemed a neat solution. Catherine herself was keen on retaining the prospect of being Queen of England, but at the time it was considered wrong for a man to marry his brother's widow, so a papal dispensation was sought.

On 23 June 1503 the twelve-year-old Henry was officially betrothed to Catherine (now seventeen years old), despite the fact that the young Henry had expressed doubts about the validity of such a marriage the year before, doubts the Archbishop of Canterbury, William Warham, shared. The dispensation arrived in April 1506 and the marriage went ahead, but not until after Henry VII's death and Henry VIII's accession to the throne in 1509.

While the account of the twists and turns of the different claims and counter-claims to the throne for the previous hundred years or so might dizzy the non-specialist reader, Henry VIII was quite clear about it all. No matter how able a king, no matter how many battles he won, no matter how successful his reign, without an heir the nation was unstable and difficult to govern, and to die without an heir meant the crown was lost. By 1527 Princess Mary, aged eleven, was Henry VIII's only surviving legitimate child—Catherine had had one stillbirth, at least one miscarriage, and one child had survived just fifty-two days. She was now forty-two years old and it is quite likely that Henry had been told that her child-bearing years were over. In any case their sexual relationship had ceased in 1524.

In theory there was nothing to stop a female inheriting the throne, but it had never happened. In the twelfth century the daughter of Henry I should have been crowned queen, but it had led to civil war—a great fear for Henry VIII. This partly accounts for his ruthlessness with his opponents; it is estimated he executed more than 50,000 people in his reign. Even if the Tudor claim to the throne was not challenged, without a son the throne would pass to Mary, his daughter by Catherine. Any subsequent marriage of hers to a member of a foreign dynasty could see the throne—and the kingdom—pass to foreign hands. All that the Tudors had fought for would be lost. Salvation was in a son.

But there was another factor. The 16th-century mind thought that events displayed the specific will of God—a will that could be interpreted. In Henry's case this meant that if he had a son God was personally endorsing his kingship—and his marriage to Catherine, papal dispensation or not. But there was no son: God must be expressing his disapproval.

All the original objections to the marriage had been based on two Bible verses, Leviticus 18:16 ('Do not have sexual relations with your brother's wife; that would dishonour your brother') and Leviticus 20:17 ('If a man marries his brother's wife, it is an act of impurity; he has dishonoured his brother. They will be childless').

Henry and Catherine had no children, or at least no sons, which amounted to the same thing to Henry, so here was certain proof of God's displeasure. Some have argued that Henry VIII's subsequent scruples about his marriage to Catherine were based solely on his desire to have Anne Boleyn. But this does not give sufficient weight to the 16th-century mindset. The fact that a papal dispensation was required clearly shows the contemporary thinking that Henry and Catherine's marriage was indeed a forbidden relationship. Secular historians of today sometimes find it difficult to grasp the reality of these spiritual issues and can lose sight of this perspective—a perspective Henry VIII certainly had. Henry was not casual in his religion—he prided himself on being a theologian. He was presumably reassured by the papal dispensation—but then, when there was no son, surely God was punishing him as Leviticus 20 said he would? This lack of a son was a double blow to Henry: his kingdom was threatened, and his marriage condemned by God.

Were Henry and the Church correct in their interpretation of these verses? Many scholars throughout Europe who were consulted said that they were, despite the instructions in Deuteronomy that seem to contradict it. Deuteronomy 25:5 says, 'If brothers are living together and one of them dies without a son, his widow must not marry outside the family. Her husband's brother shall take her and marry her and fulfil the duty of a brother-in-law to her.'

Henry considered, along with others, that Deuteronomy belonged to the ceremonial law, which applied only to Jews, not to Christians, so Leviticus stood without qualification. But the Roman Church's position was that Deuteronomy and Leviticus both applied to Christians. Leviticus was outlining the general principle and Deuteronomy was giving a single exception—when the widow of your brother was childless. Unfortunately for Henry his case fitted this exception precisely.

The correct explanation is most likely that Leviticus 18:16 is referring to a living divorced brother.[1] Obviously you cannot marry your brother's wife while she is still his wife, so the verse is saying you cannot marry your brother's wife even if she is divorced from him. He would be dishonoured on seeing his ex-wife with his own brother. Consequently it is legitimate to marry the widow of your brother, whether she is childless or not. There is no contradiction with the teaching of Deuteronomy. Furthermore the threat of childlessness in Leviticus 20 is probably referring to a legal position rather than actual childlessness. Deuteronomy 23:2 says, 'No one born of a forbidden marriage nor any of his descendants may enter the assembly of the LORD, even down to the tenth generation.'

In other words, there would be no legitimate heir to the family if the marriage was illegitimate (for example, if you had married your brother's wife while he was alive)—the children would not be considered Jewish. But none of this was the Church's view—or Henry's. What did Henry really think? Did he really believe that his marriage was outside the permitted affinity rules of Scripture, and so was null? Did he really see himself as a single man wronged by the papal dispensation and now out to save his kingdom from disintegration? Or was he simply driven by lust for Anne Boleyn, and brought all these other factors in to justify himself? In the end we have to say that only God knows; his Word says we cannot always be sure of our own motives: 'The heart is deceitful above all things and beyond cure. Who can understand it?'[2]

To get into the mind of a man who lived 500 years ago with any certainty is an impossible task. Whatever the motives, Henry had decided that Catherine must go—and it seems he made this decision before he started seriously courting Anne. In 1524 he ceased having marital relations with Catherine, and in June 1525 he made his illegitimate six-year-old son Henry Fitzroy (by an earlier mistress, Elizabeth Blount) the Duke of Richmond, with a view to him taking the throne if there was no subsequent legitimate son. By this process he appeared to be removing his daughter Mary from the succession, greatly offending Queen Catherine. This was a risky path; Henry knew that a more secure route would be an annulment of his marriage by the Pope to ensure that any son from a subsequent marriage would be considered legitimate. A barren wife, an 'illegitimate' marriage, and his love for Anne, were all factors forged together in a single purpose in Henry's mind: to part with Catherine and marry Anne Boleyn. To achieve that he had to take the battle right to the heart of the Catholic

Church, to question the pope's authority over him, and much more besides.

The questioning of the relationship between the Church and State, and specifically the repudiation of the Pope of Rome's jurisdiction over the English monarchy actually predates both Anne Boleyn and much of the Reformation. In December 1514 the body of Richard Hunne, a prosperous merchant who had been charged with heresy, was found hanged in the Bishop of London's jail. The Church said it was suicide and burned his body. The coroner's court said it was murder. Henry had to intervene and came down on the side of the coroner, asserting a king's jurisdiction in his own realm against that of the Church.

But Henry did not follow through the logic of his argument in subsequent years—until Anne Boleyn. Without her personal and ever-present support it is extremely doubtful that he would have had the courage and tenacity to make the final break with Rome. Starkey says of Henry and Anne together: 'She was the bolder one of the pair, the more radical and, arguably, the more principled. The girl from Hever … had metamorphosed into "one of the makers of history". It was an astonishing transformation.'[3]

Anne Boleyn's presence by his side sustained Henry through the six long years of argument with the Pope; hopes were raised, and hopes were dashed, until eventually Henry decided to take the matter into his own hands, with profound and lasting consequences for the nation.

Notes

1 See **Haley,** p. 292. Divorce was not unknown in Old Testament times, a perspective the Roman Catholic Church had lost, as they saw God forbidding divorce entirely.

2 Jeremiah 17:9.

3 **Starkey,** *Six wives: the queens of Henry VIII*, p. 286.

The engagement

The engagement, for that is what it seems to have been (the records show that from August 1527 Henry bought Anne an amazing number of gifts) proved a long one. It was nearly six years before they were married. As the summer of 1527 began few knew of any relationship between the King and Anne: by the end of the summer it was clear for all at court to see. It was a court that consisted of perhaps a thousand people, the whole entourage moving many times a year between the royal houses of Whitehall, Hampton Court, Windsor, Richmond, and Greenwich, the last being a favourite. In the summer a reduced number of people would 'progress' within a hundred-mile radius of London, looking for the best hunting, and staying at smaller Crown properties or with aristocratic friends, or in houses owned by the Church.

That summer the progress saw Anne and Henry together doing what both loved—hunting. Anne was an accomplished sportswoman and completely at home on a horse. The contrast between her and the older, stately, now overweight Catherine could not have escaped notice. Anne and Henry stayed for more than a month at a former Boleyn mansion just outside Chelmsford where they were joined by many of the Boleyn 'faction'.

There they deliberated the annulment, and it was decided that Cardinal Wolsey, currently on a foreign-policy initiative in France, could not be trusted to pursue it and that the matter should be handed over to his own secretary, the anti-reform Stephen Gardiner. Alarmed at the prospect of being sidelined, Wolsey began work on the annulment with a vigour not seen before. The house party broke up on 27 August leaving Henry with a new determination to press ahead with his plans to marry Anne.

When the autumn came normal political life resumed and Anne was Henry's acknowledged consort—a powerful figure at court. The winter was dominated by work on the 'great matter', with much correspondence to and from Rome, Anne spending at least some of the time at the family home at Hever; Henry was keen that his dispute over the papal dispensation was not seen to be based on his feelings for Anne.

Unfortunately, from Anne's point of view, her absence meant that Cardinal Wolsey was able to work his magic again on the King and get back in favour.

In the following June, just as Anne and Henry were to start that summer's progress, there was an outbreak of the 'sweat'. A disease unknown to modern medicine, it recurred in many summers. Its onset was sudden; it brought a high fever, stomach cramps, headaches, dizziness, and black spots. Victims usually sweated profusely, hence its name, and within hours they were usually dead. Its impact was dramatic:

London ground to a halt as businesses closed and houses were shuttered up. In four days 2,000 died. People collapsed without warning, some in opening their windows, some in playing with children in their street doors, some in one hour, many in two, it destroyed … some in sleep, some in wake, some in mirth, some in care, some fasting and some full, some busy and some idle; and in one house sometime three, sometime five, sometime more, sometime all.[1]

Henry at the best of times was a hypochondriac. He had bouts of illness, perhaps malaria, all his life. His diet was poor, consisting mainly of large quantities of meat. He was plagued with constipation, poor digestion, and haemorrhoids. After a serious accident when jousting he suffered persistent migraine headaches and had a painful leg ulcer which would not heal.

On news of the 'sweat' he fled with Catherine and the court to Waltham Abbey; Anne was sent to Hever. We can only guess what she said to Henry about being deserted in this way; he quickly wrote saying that her thoughts were 'unreasonable', and reaffirming his love for her. Still fearful he moved on to Hunsdon in Hertfordshire, but even here there was no escape— several members of his court fell ill and died within hours. Without delay he headed for Wolsey's house at Tytenhanger in the same county.

Then he got the news he was dreading: Anne was ill. Henry's chief physician was not available so he sent Dr William Butts, a medical graduate of Cambridge, who rode through the night to Hever. He confirmed the worst—she had the 'sweat'. England's future now hung in the balance. The disease was certainly no respecter of persons: Henry's favourite, Sir William Compton, had died, while George Boleyn had recovered, but Mary Boleyn's husband William Carey succumbed on 23 June. Eighteen in the Archbishop of Canterbury's household died within four hours. But Anne survived—although she had to remain at Hever for several weeks; Henry was taking no risks with his own health. Dr Butts got his reward—by Christmas he was Royal Physician with a large salary. He became a firm friend of Anne's and an unofficial spiritual advisor.

It was during this summer of 1528 that Henry finally stood up to Cardinal Wolsey, the man who had been his trusted advisor since he had come to the throne as a young man. The catalyst was the appointment of the new Abbess of Wilton in Wiltshire. Wolsey wanted Dame Isobel Jordan while Anne had proposed Dame Eleanor Carey. Dame Eleanor was the sister of William Carey—Mary Boleyn's now deceased husband. This seems an unwise recommendation by Anne in light of the two illegitimate children Dame Eleanor admitted to having.

Henry decided that neither should get the post, and instructed Wolsey to appoint a third person. Wolsey wanted his own candidate, and simply went ahead and appointed Dame Isobel. Henry wrote Wolsey a letter that cut through all the niceties of the day, pointing out to him in no uncertain terms that he had defied a specific instruction of the King. This undoubtedly marked a turning point in his relationship with the Cardinal.

Starkey says:

Henry, the playboy king, had grown up at last. He had had to. His determination to marry Anne had forced him to stand alone; it was Henry against the world. But, as usual, behind a newly strong man was a stronger woman: Anne herself. Henry was not only fighting for her, to keep and to marry her; she was helping to direct the blows and to plan the strategy.[2]

Henry forgave Wolsey, and indeed Anne herself remained at this time cordial towards him, writing him a friendly note on her return to court in late July 1528—but the incident was not forgotten, at least not by Henry. But Anne's public appearances with Henry were still spasmodic: Henry was keen not to damage his prospect of the annulment. Despite the new resolve, in many ways these years display Henry's vacillation. There was no statute law of marriage at this time, only canon law. If his union with Catherine was invalid he was a single man and was entitled to remarry—or rather, marry. When Charles Brandon married Henry's sister Mary Tudor, he had a previous marriage still intact, the Pope eventually obliging with the required retrospective annulment. If the King's brother-in-law could do it, why not the King? But Henry wanted the papal annulment before he married Anne—something he never got.

The Pope and Henry in a way shared the same problem—neither wanted to antagonize Catherine's nephew, the powerful potential ally, or enemy, Charles, King of Spain and soon to be Holy Roman Emperor. If Henry acted unilaterally (as his brother-in-law had) and displaced Catherine, this would risk Charles' displeasure, and he would undoubtedly put pressure on the Pope not to grant a retrospective annulment. Any child Henry had with Anne would be considered illegitimate—the very thing Henry wanted to avoid.

A further dilemma for the Pope was that his predecessor, Julian II, had given the dispensation for Henry's marriage to Catherine in the first place—against the widely held view in western Europe that a marriage between a man and his former sister-in-law was incest. What reason could he give for backtracking?

Like any politician in a corner the Pope sought to buy time. The issue, he said, could be settled by a papal representative (a 'legate')—and England's own Cardinal Wolsey. Cardinal Campeggio was duly despatched by the Pope with the clear remit of stretching the whole thing out as long as possible. With the help of Queen Catherine he managed to delay for some considerable time any meaningful discussion between the parties involved, until eventually he could do so no longer. A hearing—the 'legatine court'—was set up at Blackfriars on 31 May 1529. There Catherine made an impassioned speech—immortalized in Shakespeare's Henry VIII—and walked out, never to return to hear the case against her marriage. This court, unsurprisingly, failed to resolve the issue.

If the papal legate's goal was delay and prevarication, what was Cardinal Wolsey's part in all of this? He was a powerful figure in the Church; was he supporting Catherine and the Pope? Or was he backing Henry and the annulment? It does seem that, at the early stages, he was genuinely looking to help extricate Henry from his marriage and facilitate a new liaison with Anne. But whatever his motives, he seriously miscalculated the prospects of getting the annulment at the legatine court, and when the matter continued to make excruciatingly slow progress, Anne's doubts about him resurfaced. From this point their relationship would be strained. The King's desire for the annulment was as great as ever—but nobody could see a way forward.

Despite the Blackfriars setback, the summer of 1529 saw Anne and Henry enjoy an uninterrupted progress together. In the August they stayed at Waltham Abbey. There was not sufficient accommodation even for the inner circle of courtiers, which included Stephen Gardiner, Wolsey's academically brilliant secretary; he took accommodation at Waltham Cross, at the house of a Mr Cressy. There Gardiner recognized a fellow Cambridge graduate—a certain Dr Thomas Cranmer.[3] Cranmer was making a personal lifetime journey from Roman Catholic dogma to a Reformed evangelical position, in the course of which he was instrumental in producing the Thirty-nine Articles of Faith and the Prayer Book of the Church of England that were in widespread use right into the second half of the 20th century.

As they conversed that first evening Gardiner realized that Cranmer had a new angle on the 'great matter'—in his view the answer to the King's dilemma lay in the Bible, rather than in canon (Church) law. Cranmer did not share Gardiner's intellectual brilliance, but he was a careful scholar and gifted writer. He was duly asked to write a thesis on the issue of the annulment. It is not difficult to see who was behind this; he boarded at the home of Thomas Boleyn as he wrote it.

On the day this summer progress of 1529 was due to end Henry had an appointment with Eustace Chapuys, the new imperial ambassador, from whom much of the negative contemporary reporting about Anne has come down to our own times.[4] Nonetheless the ascent of the Boleyns continued apace. Thomas Boleyn, Anne's father, had already been given Durham House—a grand mansion in London traditionally occupied by the Bishop of Durham.

Meanwhile Cardinal Wolsey was in difficulty; he had allowed the soon-to-be-Emperor Charles to become the Pope's ally, so pushing further away any possibility of the annulment Henry so desperately wanted. On 9 October 1529 he was charged with praemunire (acting on behalf of a foreign power), dismissed as Lord Chancellor, and had most of his property confiscated. Wolsey had long been for Henry a sort of 16th-century Henry Kissinger, travelling abroad frequently to negotiate the maze of European politics, but it seems he had lost his sure touch—perhaps unnerved by the speed of the Boleyn rise. Now in the highest echelons of Tudor politics, Anne had undoubtedly been a key figure in the removal of the famous, powerful, and hated Wolsey.

The French ambassador du Bellay's contemporary comment on these events is revealing: 'The duke of Norfolk is made chief of the council and in his absence the duke of Suffolk, and above everyone Mademoiselle Anne.'[5] Anne was to retain this position of influence until her trial and death in 1536.

Henry had been dependent on Wolsey (who was eighteen years Henry's senior) for much of his reign to run the machinery of government—something that had never really interested the sportsman king. In his place as Lord Chancellor, Henry, rather surprisingly, appointed the famous Thomas More.[6] An arch-conservative, More wanted to defend the Church, stamp out heresy (the 'new learning'), and not get involved at all with the annulment. Nonetheless Henry used the anticlerical feeling that Cardinal Wolsey had generated to enact a number of measures in Parliament against the corruption of the priests. They included an attempt to restrict the number of priests who drew livings from an office but never visited the parish; forbade priests from keeping shops or taverns; forbade the clergy gambling, hunting, hawking, and visiting disreputable houses; and introduced heavy fines for committing gross and unnatural vices.

Meanwhile Anne had acquired a copy of William Tyndale's *The Obedience of the Christian Man and How all Christian Rulers Ought to Govern*, published in 1528. She had marked passages of special interest and shown them to Henry—despite it being a book deemed to be heretical, and banned from court by Wolsey. Tyndale's thesis was that all men should obey God's law, and that the concept of a separate authority for the pope and clergy was against the teaching of the Bible. Further, and one can imagine that this was particularly appealing to Henry, Tyndale believed that all men were subject to the earthly authority of the king, and that, in turn, the king was not subject to the separate authority of the Roman Catholic Church. (Tyndale had clear views on the Church–State relationship—as he also did about Henry's marriage to Catherine. He believed that that marriage was valid so he did not support the annulment. It is ironic that he shared this view with Thomas More, his determined persecutor.)

To bolster the case for Cranmer's new approach to the annulment—that the Bible rather than canon law should decide the matter—late in 1529 the universities of Europe were canvassed for their opinions on what Scripture said about the legality of Henry's marriage to Catherine—and whether or not the Pope could override 'Divine Law' (the Bible). The Sorbonne in Paris came up with the wrong answer, and Francis I, who was now committed to supporting Henry's case, wrote to the French parliament threatening the university with dire consequences; they duly changed their minds and supported Henry's cause. Catherine's response was that for every academic coming out on the side of Henry she would find a thousand to support her argument.

Chapuys records that in the November, when Henry reported this latest comment of Catherine's, Anne told Henry that she had wasted her youth waiting for him, only to have him wilt each time Catherine argued with him. The conversation is uncorroborated, but that December, perhaps by way of consolation, in a ceremony in Wolsey's confiscated York Place, Thomas Boleyn was created Earl of Wiltshire and Earl of Ormonde, and in the New Year made Lord Privy Seal—the third highest office in the land, an office normally reserved for a churchman. The secularization of the Church assets and income had begun. Anne was now Lady Rochford and George, Lord Rochford—he was also given a place in the Privy Council. Catherine still attended all the formal state occasions, but Anne was now an unofficial queen in waiting.

Notes

1 Quoted by **Denny,** p. 117.
2 **Starkey,** *Six wives: the queens of Henry VIII*, p. 336.

3 See Appendix 4: Biographical sketches.

4 Ibid.

5 **Ives,** *The Life and Death of Anne Boleyn*, p. 126.

6 See Appendix 4: Biographical sketches.

A queen in waiting

After dismissing Wolsey as Chancellor, Henry allowed him to retire to York, where, in early 1530, he saw for the first time the diocese for which he had held the archbishopric for sixteen years. He began to devote himself to religious duties, but his love of power would not go away. In February 1530 Charles V had been crowned Holy Roman Emperor by Pope Clement VII and there was renewed hope that Europe would be unified in its Catholicism. Seeing an opportunity Wolsey entered into correspondence to align himself in a new understanding with Catherine, Charles V, and Rome—in other words, choosing to act against Henry and his 'great matter', bringing together the old Catholic forces against change and reform. In April 1530 he contacted Chapuys to broker this new deal. But in the October, letters from Wolsey's agent Agostini addressed to the court of Rome were intercepted; some of the text was in cipher. Wolsey's new treasonable plot was exposed.

This was the last straw for Anne; she so forcibly presented her view of this latest development that Henry was driven to tears (male tears not being unfashionable at this time). Wolsey was summoned from the north of England to be interrogated, but died on the way of natural causes in November 1530.

Meanwhile Thomas Boleyn had been despatched by Henry to meet the Pope and the newly crowned Charles V at Bologna to press again for the annulment. The meeting did not go well, and Thomas stated that England might well declare its independence from Rome—a declaration, he said, that would be imitated by other kingdoms. The following month at Augsburg evangelical factions in northern Germany, addressed by Martin Luther, united in protest against the Catholic Church, gaining the name 'Protestant'.

The Pope's reply to Thomas Boleyn was a fine of 10,000 ducats on Henry and a threat of excommunication if he married without the Church's permission. This seems to have unnerved Henry; a new commission was set up to assess religious reform and Henry declared that the Bible in English might for Christians 'rather be to their confusion and destruction than the edification of their souls'.[1]

However, other books appeared that challenged the traditional role of the Church and the authority of the Pope. Henry grew in confidence and royal policy became more radical again. The ruling body (or 'parliament') of the Church of Rome in England was the Convocation of the province of Canterbury. In February 1531 Henry demanded that they recognize him as 'sole protector and Supreme Head of the English Church and clergy'. The arguments went to and fro, George Boleyn, Anne's brother, playing a leading part. Eventually Convocation caved in to Henry's demand, as long as the words 'so far as the law of Christ allows' were inserted. As each side of the argument could interpret in their own way what actually the 'law of Christ' did allow, this became a happy (but obviously flawed) compromise.

As on previous occasions, Henry didn't follow through with the new agreement hammered out with Convocation. He still wanted, and fought for, his papal annulment. Henry was never an evangelical: he was not a radical, rather he died a Roman Catholic by conviction. He embraced the arguments of the 'new learning' as long as they took him in the direction he wanted to go—but he lacked the personal conviction of Anne, or of others at court, who had come to realize that the Scriptures really are the sole authority for men and women in this life.

Also, Henry was a political realist, as was his future daughter Elizabeth. He knew that any French alliance with Charles V and the Pope would leave England isolated, and that this was far more likely to occur if England went alone against the rest of Christendom. Further, he knew that there was a limit to the measures for which he could secure popular consent at home; England was still very much a Catholic country.

Although Anne and Henry now spent much of their time together, this was not a happy time. The annulment was no nearer—the King's 'great matter' was still bogged down. Further appeals were made to Catherine to agree to have the case settled in England, but with no success. Anne was now thirty, and there are stories of her being waspish and difficult. Some care needs to be taken with these accounts, as to whose opinion is being quoted, but she could be sharp-tongued. Certainly no one ever accused her of being shy and retiring—certainly not Henry—but his love for her did not diminish no matter how she might chide him. Her impatience is understandable: the position was clear as far as she could see. Anne had come to believe Tyndale's arguments about a monarch's authority, so what was to stop Henry assuming his rightful authority and declaring his marriage null as he believed it to be? But most at court were with Henry, in that they wanted an annulment agreed by Catherine and endorsed by the Pope, rather than the alternative—a radical break with Rome. Catherine, unsurprisingly, was determined to hang on to her marriage. The main plank of her defence was that her marriage to Arthur, Henry's brother, had never been consummated. It was, she claimed, never a real marriage—therefore she had been free to marry Henry notwithstanding any papal dispensation. Few were convinced, despite Catherine swearing on oath to it before several worthy Church dignitaries.

In retrospect it can be seen that the most important event of this time was the rise of Thomas Cromwell.[2] For fourteen years he had worked for Cardinal Wolsey, yet he had managed to survive the Cardinal's fall from favour. By the opening of 1531 he was a member of the Privy Council. It was probably Cromwell who came up with the compromise formula 'as far as the law of Christ allows', the spoonful of sugar that allowed Convocation to swallow the unpalatable statement that Henry 'was Supreme Head of the English Church and clergy'. In Cromwell the evangelicals at court had a new champion, an able and clever politician; one who within a few short years, however, was to turn against them with devastating effect.

Parliament met in January 1532. There were several draft bills put to it by Henry and his counsellors, some pursuing the line of independence from Rome, others seeking to bring pressure on Rome for the annulment. One idea was to stop the practice whereby those newly appointed to a paid office of the Church in England made payments to the Pope (annates) for the benefit received. This measure would enable Henry to keep the payments for himself if there was a split with Rome. The bill faced vigorous opposition in both Houses of Parliament—Henry was not in for a smooth ride.

Cromwell, eager to find a solution to the King's 'great matter' and so make his way in court, could see that the only solution was to push the King along the more radical route: forget the papal annulment—the Pope was not for turning; instead make a decisive break with Rome. Most in England were orthodox in belief—after all, the vast majority knew no different—but this does not mean that the Church or its clergy were popular. There had been growing unrest at the increasing number of persecutions for heresy instituted by the new Lord Chancellor Thomas More. Famously known for his desire to act according to his conscience when he refused to endorse Henry's rejection of Catherine, Thomas More vigorously persecuted others who wished to act according to their own conscience and embrace the evangelical faith. He instituted the first burnings for heresy for more than fifteen years.

Complaints about these executions became more frequent in the House of Commons. Cromwell again showed his political skill by choosing this time to have submitted to Parliament a bill drafted by him: 'Supplication against the Ordinaries'. Although it was buried in the legalese, the bottom line was that the Church had to decide who was 'boss'—the Pope or the King. Convocation chose Stephen Gardiner to reply. The King's secretary, the intellectually gifted Gardiner would have been a good choice, but he had been out of the country some weeks so was somewhat out of the loop. He believed that the traditionalists at this point were in the ascendancy and so blithely reasserted the old arguments about the Church's authority, despite Convocation having already conceded that Henry was indeed its 'Supreme Head'. Gardiner had completely misread the King's mood and growing impatience.

Henry lost it. The years of frustration had taken their toll and he angrily started to throw his weight around. On 15 May 1532 Parliament was dismissed and the same day Convocation was ordered to adjourn—but only after giving the King the assurance he had sought about his position as head of the Church in England, now asserted without reservation. Thomas More gave up his seal of office, and Warham, the Archbishop of Canterbury, knew the fight was over.

Cromwell was obviously the man of the moment and his star was rising. The Duke of Norfolk, Anne's uncle, was counted among the winners in the debacle, but he was in an ambivalent position. He stood for tradition and the Roman Catholic Church; he favoured the path of pressure on Rome, rather than the radical break with the Pope that Cromwell wanted. But

Norfolk also enjoyed the power and influence of his position at court, and to further that he wanted to see his niece as queen. Anne's growing confidence, her independence of mind, and her evangelical views were all, however, rather large flies in the ointment—it was not long before he presided over the trial that sent Anne to her death. Others tried to adjust to the blunt shift in the landscape of power politics at court that the fall of Thomas More and Cardinal Wolsey had brought about. Stephen Gardiner gave up one of his properties (Hanworth) to Anne Boleyn to try to make amends for his mistake. But it was too late. Henry never trusted him in the same way again, although it was another three years before he stepped down from being the King's secretary.

Anne's influence was now clear for all to see. Often people appealed to her directly for help in securing some appointment, or to intervene in some dispute. Any person in such a position of influence is likely to attract negative comment and Anne was no exception. It was reported at this time that she refused to intercede when a young priest was to be executed for tampering with coins, making the comment that there were too many priests already. This is similar to her alleged remark that she wished that all Spaniards were at the bottom of the sea. Certainly Anne could be sharp-tongued, too sharp for many, but there is no objective evidence that she ever made either statement.

In the summer of 1532 Henry and Anne faced another obstacle. Henry Percy, the young man who had fallen in love with her when she first arrived back in England, was still weathering his subsequent unhappy marriage. His wife, in a bid to extricate herself from it, began to claim that there had been a marriage pre-contract between Anne and Percy—in other words, that her husband was really married to Anne. Anne's opponents seized on this, but in her usual robust manner, when she got wind of it she went straight to the King and insisted the matter be thoroughly investigated. Henry Percy was interrogated on oath by two archbishops, and then in the presence of many witnesses swore on the consecrated emblems of the Mass that no pre-contract ever existed.

In 1532 Henry stepped up his gifts to Anne, including an open-sleeved cloak of black satin, a black satin nightgown, and a gown in green damask—clothes suitable for a queen, and which she wore with suitable panache. Preparations were started for a coronation, the whole thing being given added impetus by the timely death (at least from Henry's point of view) of Warham, the elderly Archbishop of Canterbury. Cranmer, clearly in the Boleyn camp, was named as his successor.

For Anne's proposed new role she needed status in her own right. At an impressive ceremony at Windsor Castle on 1 September 1532 she knelt before Henry and was granted the title of Marquis of Pembroke, along with its associated lands and income. An indication of the uncertainty of the times was that the wording of the documents relating to the title was changed so that any son born to her would inherit the title even if born outside lawful marriage. Henry was taking no chances over any challenges he might face concerning the legitimacy of his eventual marriage to Anne.

Then, as today, a successful foreign trip by a leader could be used to bolster a difficult domestic situation, so Henry planned a trip to France with his prospective queen. Furthermore Henry thought that during his stay in France he could persuade Francis I to support his marriage to Anne, providing England with an important ally against Charles V if he proved difficult about the annulment of Henry's marriage to his aunt. The arrangements for the trip did not go smoothly at first as many at the French court were not sure how to react to Henry's proposed annulment and remarriage. Anne played a key part in ensuring that the plans went well, the French ambassador recognizing her role in this, saying to Chapuys, the imperial ambassador, that her services to France were more than could ever be repaid.

On Friday 11 October Henry and Anne took a ship from Dover to Calais (at that time an English territory). She had left France ten years previously a lady-in-waiting; she returned with the guns of the royal salute echoing in everybody's ears, the local dignitaries parading out to greet her, her intended husband at her side. She spent ten days in Calais with Henry, to all appearances as his queen. Then Henry left for Boulogne to meet with Francis I, bringing the French monarch back to Calais with him on Friday 25 October. Francis had already sent a diamond worth £3,000 as a present for Anne, but she was nowhere to be seen when he arrived. He could hardly be missed; they fired 3,000 guns in his honour. But Anne knew her stuff. On the Sunday night Henry prepared a great banquet—elaborate cloth hangings, thousands of glittering candles, 170 dishes prepared alternately in French and English style.

At the climax Anne made her entry, leading six women, all wearing masks, all 'gorgeously apparelled', in a 'strange fashion'.[3] They each chose a man to dance with, Anne choosing Francis. Eventually Henry could contain his childlike excitement no more—this was just the sort of event he loved. He insisted the masks came off, and his wife-to-be was revealed. Anne danced on with her ladies for a further hour, then spent some considerable time talking with the French king, using her fluency in the language to advantage.

Francis left Calais on 29 October while Henry and Anne stayed on for a few more days as they had intended. Severe weather, however, delayed their eventual departure until 12 November. They arrived safely in Dover but only reached London after several more days. It is known that between Francis I leaving Calais and the arrival of Henry and Anne back in London, after so many years of waiting, Anne finally agreed to sleep with Henry. Their relationship was consummated.

Why did Anne agree to this, before Henry was 'divorced', and before they were married? But was not Henry in her eyes already single? Anne and Henry were agreed, mistakenly, that Leviticus 20:17 meant that Henry should not have married his sister-in-law. That marriage was invalid—or so they thought—and therefore Henry was a single man. All that Henry was waiting for was a papal decree to say so. But Anne did not believe that the Pope stood in Christ's place on earth, speaking with Christ's authority—he was not, as he claimed, 'The Vicar of Christ on earth'. Consequently she did not believe the Pope had the right to give the final word on Henry's marriage; it was up to Henry himself to make the decision, him having already been declared by the Church's own Convocation to be head of the Church in England. As has been seen, whether or not all this was Henry's personal conviction cannot be known.

But this is certainly what he wanted. What was stopping him declaring on the marriage? Was it that he was not fully persuaded? Or could it be that the political difficulties he envisaged if he did declare his marriage null were holding him back? Anne, however, could marry Henry with a clear conscience. In her understanding of the Scriptures Henry was free to marry. It was an understanding many contemporary scholars endorsed.

If they were free to marry, why didn't Anne wait for a proper marriage ceremony—especially after waiting more than six years already? The state registration of marriages only began in England in 1857; until then marriages were controlled by the Church. Myles Coverdale (the Bible translator of the latter part of Henry VIII's reign) stated in *The Christen State of Matrymonye* that it was possible to contract a marriage, often with a 'handfasting' ceremony (where the couple literally tied their hands together), and then have a separate wedding service performed in a church several weeks after the consummation of the relationship. The Church fully accepted this position.

As seen in Chapter 4 the emphasis in the 16th century was on the commitment and the consummation; the ceremony might follow later. If this seems puzzling, consider baptism. Today some Christians believe that this should precede a profession of faith and therefore they baptize infant children. But others believe baptism should follow a profession of faith. In the latter case, a baptism is conducted at some stage subsequent to conversion as a public declaration of what has happened. This is similar to the two views that were held in the 16th century about the marriage service. A public ceremony could be conducted before, or after, the consummation of the relationship. If after, the ceremony was a public display that the marriage had taken place. It would not be considered immoral for a couple to contract a marriage between themselves—even to consummate it—before the ceremony in the church. Obviously this could lead to misunderstandings and eventually the practice was adopted whereby the ceremony came first. But nonetheless it is important to understand that in the early 16th century a private commitment and consummation could properly take place before any formal church ceremony—it was accepted practice.

There is circumstantial evidence to suggest that it was Henry's intention to marry Anne with a public ceremony in Calais with Francis present, but Francis had persuaded him against this. If so, the collapse of the plans for a wedding in Calais was a further setback for Anne and Henry and would only have increased their frustration. Was the situation for them anything like that portrayed in the popular film about Anne Boleyn, *Anne of the*

1000 days?4 At a climactic moment in the film, in frustration and anger, Henry pleads with Anne, asking what more he has to do before she will consent to be his bride. Certainly Henry had antagonized friends and enemies at home and abroad for her sake. He had sacked and even executed loyal servants. He had caused divisions in his family. He had looked to cast aside the Pope and the historic teachings of the Church. He had paraded her as his queen in Calais for the world to see—all for his love of her. You can imagine him saying, 'What more do you want?'

You can further imagine Anne saying, 'Have the marriage to Catherine declared null.' And it is probable that Henry made just that promise. To Anne it would have been a believable promise; she knew Thomas Cranmer was going to be the new Archbishop of Canterbury, and he was firmly in the Boleyn camp and favoured the break with Rome. It would indeed have proved to be a promise fulfilled. The following May Henry's marriage to Catherine was declared to be null by the new archbishop.

What could Anne have done? She must have realized that this was the moment—she could hold out no longer. She finally agreed to consummate her relationship with Henry VIII, who had never lost his fascination for her through all the long years of the engagement, much to the astonishment of everybody at court. Furthermore it appears that there was indeed a ceremony; the 16th-century chronicler Edward Hall says: 'The king, after his return [from Calais] married privily the Lady Anne Bulleyn on Saint Erkenwald's Day [Thursday 14 November 1532], which marriage was kept so secret, that very few knew it, till she was great with child, at Easter after.'5

The Elizabethan apologist Nicholas Sander, who wrote against the break from Rome, and therefore would have reason to cast doubt on Elizabeth's legitimacy, similarly named 14 November as Anne and Henry's wedding day.6 It appears that this ceremony was conducted immediately on landing in Dover, possibly without a priest present—although Starkey thinks Anne would have insisted on that as well.7 After resisting such monumental pressure for so long, would Anne have given way to Henry without such a formal, albeit secret, ceremony? There is no basis to doubt the accounts of Hall or Sander—they fit all the known facts—or to doubt that Anne was not a virgin right up to this point. If there was any prospect of proving any sexual immorality on Anne's part before the marriage to Henry, the Church of Rome could have used this to weaken significantly Anne's claim to be Henry's legitimate wife. Anne was surrounded by many enemies at court; it should have been easy to establish, or simply to make the accusation. It is a path the Pope never pursued. The testimony of history is that Anne held out for six years for a proper marriage—against one of the most powerful men in history, who prided himself on his sexual prowess.

The ceremony was performed; within weeks Anne was pregnant.

Notes

1 Quoted by **Denny,** p. 160.

2 See Appendix 4: Biographical sketches.

3 **Ives,** *The Life and Death of Anne Boleyn*, p. 160.

4 1969 Universal Pictures.

5 Quoted by **Ives,** *The Life and Death of Anne Boleyn*, p. 170.

6 Ibid.

7 **Starkey,** *Six wives: the queens of Henry VIII*, p. 463.

A queen crowned

On 25 January 1533 a more formal wedding ceremony was conducted, but still in private. It is thought the ceremony took place before dawn over the Holbein Gate of Whitehall.[1] The priest asked if Henry had the Pope's permission; Henry replied somewhat disingenuously that he had a document giving him licence to marry. It is true that Henry did have a licence from the Pope to marry Anne Boleyn, but it was conditional upon the declaration that his marriage to Catherine was void. It did not specify who would make that declaration; ultimately Cranmer did.

Why did Henry still feel it necessary to keep this wedding ceremony a secret? Because he knew he was still not in the clear. Anne's uncle, the Duke of Norfolk, an influential figure at court, had gone with the flow because it suited him, but there were signs that he was not happy with this new radical approach of a break with Rome. Charles Brandon, Henry's brother-in-law, was openly hostile. Henry could not be confident, either, about domestic popular opinion. Many in the country had a sense of 'fair play'; they would not be happy about Henry putting aside his wife of more than twenty years. Also, Henry never lost his desire to have a papal annulment of his marriage to Catherine. This is understandable, not just for political reasons: he had spent a lifetime as a Roman Catholic, and he eventually died one. It must have been a tremendous wrench in his conscience to go against the 'Vicar of Christ'.

But within weeks Anne knew that she was pregnant and things moved on apace. On 14 March Thomas Cromwell presented a bill before Parliament, 'The Act of Appeals', which would put on the statute book a statement of royal supremacy and so make the break with Rome. On 26 March Convocation (the Church's parliament) was asked to pronounce on the invalidity of the papal dispensation that had enabled Henry to marry Catherine. On 30 March, Thomas Cranmer was consecrated as Archbishop of Canterbury. Within days the relevant procedures finally to resolve the 'great matter' had been pushed through Convocation and Parliament. Henry's marriage was declared null and Catherine was told to change her title to that of dowager Princess of Wales.

Finally on Easter Sunday 1533 Anne went to Mass as Henry's wife and de facto queen. (At this stage few evangelicals saw attending Mass as a problem. The big issue was 'justification by faith'. It was only after Anne's death that the Catholic teaching on the Mass became a matter of contention for the Reformers.) Wearing a crown and glittering with jewellery she had sixty maids of honour and her train was carried by her cousin. Queen Anne was prayed for by name.

Coronation day was to be Sunday, 1 June 1533; a magnificent display of wealth and power was planned. Everything was to be done by 'The Royal Book' which laid down the procedures for a coronation. Henry was determined to follow it to the letter, although some innovations were allowed. The celebrations were to be spread over four days, and on Thursday 29 May Anne was brought by water from Greenwich to the Tower of London (still a royal palace—not the prison we think of now). There was much pageantry, both on the streets of London and on the river, where many large barges had been prepared with covered cabins, all decorated with flags and bunting. One boat had a mechanical dragon on board that moved and belched out flames; others had models of monsters, and huge 'wild men' who threw blazing fireworks. Some had musicians and singers, and there were others with dignitaries on board, keen not to miss being seen in the great river parade.

Anne had her own barge, powered by twenty-four oars and lavishly decorated, and with her were the principal ladies of court. Another barge followed behind carrying the rest of her women, and behind that the King's barge with all his guard in their finest uniforms, along with royal trumpeters and minstrels. Ships in the Pool of London joined in with the official gun salutes. It was a great display, and when Henry welcomed Anne at the Tower, he could not help but show his pleasure. Anne and Henry stayed the night and all next day in the newly reconstructed apartments in the south-east corner. On Friday evening Henry made eighteen men Knights of the Bath (the postulants literally having to take a bath the night before), an honour normally associated with the coronation of a king. What did the general public make of all this? There was undoubted sympathy for Catherine, and some were surely antagonistic to Anne. But the King had got his way, it was a dazzling display of wealth and power, and many hoped that Anne would provide Henry with the son who would secure the succession and give the nation a settled future.

The weather for the procession to Westminster on Saturday 31 May was perfect. The route was lined by various displays, the public held back by a line of marshals. Despite the unscheduled late start—5 p.m.—it was another display of well-ordered pomp and glamour. The procession was headed by twelve servants of the new French ambassador, then came the gentlemen of the royal households, followed by nine judges in their scarlet gowns and hoods. Next came the new Knights of the Bath, the royal council, the ecclesiastical magnates, and peers of the realm. The presence of the new ambassador of France was crucial, signifying French support; the Venetian ambassador was also there.

The Lord Mayor also processed—as did Charles Brandon, the King's brother-in-law, wisely choosing to show his support, at least outwardly. Some absented themselves: Mary Tudor; Anne's aunt, the Duke of Norfolk's wife; and notably Thomas More, although he took the £20 allowance for the gown he was supposed to wear. Within the year he was in the Tower; he was eventually executed in 1535.

Finally came Anne herself. She was dressed in white cloth of gold edged in ermine. Bare-headed as tradition dictated, her unfashionably dark hair was on display for all to see, drawing special comment from Cranmer. Her litter was decked out in white cloth of gold, and was drawn by two small horses clothed to the ground in white damask. Over her was a canopy of silk to match her carriage, held up by the barons of the Cinque Ports (five historic ports that had special Crown-granted privileges—Hastings, New Romney, Hythe, Dover, and Sandwich). Twelve ladies in crimson velvet rode behind her, and then followed two carriages decked in red cloth of gold, seven more riders, two more carriages … and so on. Henry knew how to show off, and he was determined to show off his new queen in a grand fashion—a queen for whom he had waited so many years. Crowds lined the streets and hung out of windows, their cheers mingling with the sound of trumpets and cannon fire. At certain points the procession would stop so that Anne could receive gifts, hear choirs, or watch amazing pageants. The first stop was at Fenchurch Street, where children dressed as merchants welcomed Anne—a reference to her wide contacts with the merchant community. Poets sympathetic to reform had written verses to celebrate the coronation of their new evangelical queen. At the gate of St Paul's Churchyard was an empty throne—waiting, as it were, for Anne. Beneath were three tablets carrying biblical texts: on the left was 'In the Lord I take refuge' (Psalm 11:1); on the right, 'Direct my footsteps according to your word' (Psalm 119:133); and the centre had the text 'Come my love! You shall be crowned'. This last text has no precise biblical provenance, but at the time would have been seen as a clear reference to Esther 2:17: '… So he [King Xerxes] set a royal crown on her head and made her queen instead of Vashti.'

Already parallels were being drawn between Queen Catherine, first wife of Henry, and Queen Vashti, first wife of King Xerxes; and between Queen Anne and Queen Esther, who in the biblical account went to the unbelieving king to save her people.

Having arrived at Westminster Hall, Anne stayed the Saturday night at York Place with Henry. Many wondered whether Anne, almost six months pregnant, could maintain the impression of effortless glamour throughout the coronation ceremony the next day at Westminster Abbey. They need not have doubted. Anne excelled in these set pieces of royalty when the display of pomp and ceremony was all-important, as did her daughter Elizabeth years later. Both women would have been a gift to any modern image-maker employed by a royal family.

She arrived at Westminster Hall at 9 a.m. on Sunday 1 June and processed along a walkway carpeted in blue for the 700 yards from the Hall to the High Altar of the Abbey, wearing robes of purple velvet lined with ermine, and, as The Royal Book demanded, 'bareheaded and bare-visaged … that all men may behold her'. The gold canopy was carried over her, and before her the Lord Great Chamberlain carried the crown. Everything was done according to the correct protocol—Henry did not want to make any mistakes.

Special stands had been erected in the Abbey, including one for the King where he could watch proceedings hidden behind a latticework screen. This was Anne's day and he did not want to steal her thunder. Mass was said, and at the climax of events Anne was anointed and then crowned by Archbishop Cranmer with the crown of St Edward—an honour normally reserved for a reigning monarch, not the monarch's consort. The pomp and ceremony had worked their magic—she really was now the queen.

They returned to Westminster Hall, where a lavish and magnificent banquet for more than 800 guests was held. Anne sat alone at a long marble table on the King's large marble chair mounted on a dais. The Archbishop of Canterbury, the only person to share the table with her, was some way off to the right. Nothing was to detract from the focus of the day—Queen Anne. Charles Brandon had responsibility for the event. He wore a jacket draped with pearls, and rode around on a horse which itself was dressed in crimson velvet. Lord William Howard (another of Anne's uncles) assisted, also riding a suitably attired horse. The two of them escorted in, on horseback, the first course of the banquet. At the end of a long afternoon Anne gave her thanks and presented to the Mayor of London a commemorative gold cup. Her own coronation medal was issued, stamped with the legend 'The Most Happy'.

Anne and Henry spent the post-coronation 'honeymoon' at Greenwich, as, with the Tower and York Place, this had been extensively refurbished for Anne. Eventually they went by water to York Place, then to Windsor on 17 July. From there Henry went hunting, despite on 11 July the Pope having excommunicated him—casting him, as the Church believed, into eternal darkness. The Duke of Norfolk, Anne's uncle, was said to have fainted on hearing the news. But the die had been cast; there was no going back. Anne soon settled down to her new life at court as the King's official consort.

The Royal Book did not specify how long before a birth a queen should retreat to her confinement suite, but it was usual to do so some weeks before the due date. The baby Elizabeth was born on Sunday, 7 September 1533, so Anne's confinement proved to be short. Was there perhaps some confusion about the dates? Also, everybody, especially Henry, had been confidently predicting a son; somewhat naively Henry had had all the documents drawn up with the word 'prince', but now all had to be duly modified. There was great disappointment, and some of the public celebrations were abandoned. But to temper Henry's disappointment, Anne had survived and there was a healthy baby daughter. The Roman Catholic Church, then and now, believed that unbaptized babies were at risk of not entering heaven, so the christening was carried out quickly, on 10 September, with a magnificent ceremony, which according to the custom of the time neither parent attended.[2] Archbishop Cranmer was named as the godfather.

Elizabeth was taken back to her parents, but then placed in the nursery suite at Greenwich to be cared for by others. There is subsequently little further mention of Anne's daughter, although it is known that Anne took what for the time was a very close interest in her upbringing. At three months Elizabeth was sent to be fostered at Hertford where Anne visited regularly; she was in frequent touch with Lady O'Brien who was in charge of the child's care. But in the tradition of the day the child was not seen as Anne's responsibility, but that of Henry and his Council. They made all the important decisions about what was to happen to Elizabeth—even the date she was weaned. Later, when Anne was close to death, it was clear that Elizabeth was supremely important to her, but it is difficult to know what specific influence she had on her daughter.

In the immediate aftermath of the birth Henry and Anne maintained their public cheerfulness, but there was no getting round the fact that a son would have consolidated Anne's position in a way that a daughter did not. She was still vulnerable, and Henry still anxious about the succession. No matter how beautiful, how charismatic, how well dressed; no matter how talented at singing, dancing, and playing musical instruments; no matter how intelligent, how well educated: a queen's principal duty was to produce a son. Anne had ascended to the highest position in the land with a remarkable combination of skills and courage, but if she failed in this one thing, she had failed completely. Anne knew this, as did Henry—as too did all those hostile to the marriage and the break with the Pope. Some reported that the King's ardour for Anne cooled after this latest setback. However, there is no evidence for this—his love for her appears to have been as strong as ever.

But the new family dynamics created additional tensions with respect to Henry's daughter Mary, now seventeen years old. She stubbornly refused to be the dutiful daughter and accept the new half-sister Elizabeth. Most thought that Anne was to blame for the poor relationship with Mary, and that Henry was an innocent bystander. But this was not the case, as was clearly demonstrated after Anne's death, when Henry treated Mary more harshly than Anne had ever been accused of.

This is not to say that Anne did not have her moments and lose her temper with the truculent Mary from time to time; however, there is no evidence that there was ever any attempt to harm her: stories of Anne plotting to poison her are a fiction. Anne sought to establish a good relationship with Mary, but she always insisted that she acknowledge her as the rightful queen, something that Mary adamantly refused to do, choosing instead to refer to Anne as her father's mistress. Mary's negative reaction was understandable—she had seen Anne depose her mother and at this time she believed she herself had lost any claim to the throne of England to her new half-sister. Any reader who has had experience of teenage children, let alone an aggrieved stepchild, can perhaps understand the problem that the two women had in relating to each other.

In March 1534 the Pope finally pronounced on Henry's marriage, in Catherine's favour—but it was not on the terms she wanted. There was not even a mention of the claimed non-consummation of her first marriage to Arthur, Henry's brother. In the same month the Act of Succession was passed in England; this stated precisely the opposite of the announcement from Rome, and Catherine had her title confirmed as Princess Dowager. The heir to the throne was to be any male heir of Henry's by Anne, or by any subsequent wife.

Early in 1534 Anne was pregnant again, but hopes were dashed when just before the time came for her official confinement, probably in the July when perhaps only seven months into her pregnancy, she went into labour and lost the baby. This was another setback for the couple, and Henry went on the summer progress alone, although Anne did manage to join him later.

In September 1534 Pope Clement died, to be replaced by Paul III. There was hope in England of reconciliation—but it was not to be. The new pope upheld the validity of Henry's original marriage to Catherine, meaning that Anne was not Henry's lawful wife. In response, in the autumn Cromwell pushed through a series of parliamentary Acts to make non-recognition of the new royal status quo a treasonable offence, firstly in the Act of Supremacy, where Henry was declared to be Supreme Head of the

Church in England, and then in the Act of Treasons. Henry had given up using Scripture exposition to win hearts and minds—it was now to be the axe. These were uncertain times; it was in the October of 1534 that the terrible persecutions (referred to in Chapter 3) began in France with the 'night of the placards', and in the following January there was a mass execution in France of evangelical Christians, Francis I himself attending the spectacle.

Following on from the parliamentary legislation of that autumn, in the spring of 1535 the deaths came to England as well. The victims were deliberately chosen so as to make the maximum impact on those previously not persuaded by Henry's logic. Four leading monks were hung, drawn, and quartered.[3] Then, to show an even-handedness, twenty-three Protestants, refugees from the Low Countries who had fled to England for safety, were arrested. They were Anabaptists, who believed, as many evangelicals do today, that baptism was for those who had made a profession of faith. But this was not the orthodoxy of the day, and fourteen were burnt at the stake.

In June the devout Bishop of Rochester, John Fisher, newly appointed a cardinal on Catherine's recommendation, was beheaded on Tower Hill, provoking outrage in Catholic Europe. Henry was excommunicated for the second time. England now had Spain, France, and the papacy ranged against it. There were plans to depose Henry, replace him with his daughter Mary, and restore England to the Catholic fold. Undoubtedly it was envisaged that Mary would then marry a European Catholic prince who would duly claim the crown of England. In July Sir Thomas More, like his fellow churchman Fisher, was also beheaded. Naturally none of these events helped Anne's cause—particularly the latter, many seeing her as some sort of latter-day Salome (the daughter of Herodias whose dancing impressed Herod so much he was willing to give her John the Baptist's head). As a further setback, it appears that at about this time Anne had another miscarriage.

Despite all this Henry seemed in good spirits. Chapuys reports that days after More's execution he was still celebrating as he set off with Anne on the usual summer progress. Perhaps aware of the public relations' damage of recent events they planned that this progress was going to be a 'meet the people'—especially those who might be sympathetic to Anne and the reforms she stood for. And many were, especially in London and the south-west, particularly Bristol. The progress met with some success; Chapuys somewhat gloomily had to report that the King and Queen were 'gaining the people … that many of the peasants where [Henry] has passed, hearing the preachers who follow the Court, are so much abused as to believe that God has inspired the King to separate himself from the wife of his brother.'[4]

Among those visited were Sir John and Lady Walsh; the live-in tutor to their children had been none other than William Tyndale. From him had come this couple's love of the gospel.

At this time Cromwell was all-powerful, managing affairs back at the heart of government when not actually present with the royal progress. Undoubtedly Anne was exercising considerable influence, Starkey says of this progress: 'And, throughout, [Cromwell's] most active co-adjutor was Anne herself. She managed Henry; wrote to Cromwell on his absences from Court, and, where necessary, took the initiative on the ground.'[5]

To crown a successful summer, on 19 September, in Winchester Cathedral, three new evangelical bishops were consecrated: Foxe of Hereford, Latimer of Worcester, and Hilsey of Rochester.[6] Anne had secured their appointments through her personal influence, working tirelessly to remove the many obstacles that were put in their way. Almost certainly Anne and Henry were present at their consecration.

Notes

1 Henry VIII had acquired York Place from Cardinal Wolsey, transforming it into Whitehall Palace. It was largely destroyed by fire in 1698, only the Banqueting House surviving.

2 'The Church can only entrust them to the mercy of God … to hope that there is a way of salvation for children who have died without baptism'. Catechism of the Catholic Church 1261, quoted by **Kreeft,** p. 312. It does not seem that the statement by Pope Benedict XVI in April 2007 has changed this position.

3 Victims were dragged on a wooden frame to the place of execution, then hung by the neck, but taken down before death and disembowelled. The genitalia and entrails were burned before the victims' eyes, then they were beheaded, and the body divided into four parts.

4 **Starkey,** Six wives: the queens of Henry VIII, p. 532.

5 Ibid. p. 526.

6 Hugh Latimer was the Bishop of Worcester; William Latymer was a chaplain to Anne—confusingly his name is sometimes spelt Latimer.

A queen under pressure

In September 1535, during the summer progress, Anne and Henry stopped at Wolf Hall near Marlborough, the home of Sir John Seymour. His eldest daughter Jane might have been present—her eldest brother, Edward, protégé of the deceased Cardinal Wolsey, was a rising star at court. But it is unlikely at this time that the King took any particular interest in Jane; Henry and Anne still seemed very much the couple in love. Within weeks of this meeting Anne was pregnant again—the royal marriage appeared to be as strong as ever. But there were external difficulties. Many still resented Catherine being put to one side, and wanted Mary reinstated as the rightful heir to the throne. Some participated in public demonstrations to that end—one was even led by Anne's own aunt, Lady William Howard, and Anne's sister-in-law Jane, wife of George. Jane Boleyn never shared the evangelical convictions of Anne and George.

In the country there was a widespread fear of religious change. Cromwell's deputies were confiscating Church relics and 1 December was the date set for a new ten per cent tax on clerical incomes. There was rumour of an impending war with Charles V—indeed Catherine had written directly to him asking him to intervene on her behalf. What is more, the weather in England was exceptionally wet and the harvest that autumn was delayed. A combination of trouble at home and abroad, a rise in taxes, and that most feared of all things, change, made the situation difficult for Henry and Anne.

Then just after Christmas, on 7 January 1536, Catherine died unexpectedly. Henry's relief, and that of the Boleyn faction at court, was demonstrable. Henry was 'like one transported with joy', saying, 'God be praised that we are free from all suspicion of war', and he proceeded to carry around Elizabeth, now a toddler, to display to his friends. Far from mourning he dressed in bright yellow and decided to celebrate by doing two of the things he loved most—eating and jousting.[1] A banquet and jousting tournament were quickly arranged. While the high spirits overtly expressed over the next days seem callous, Catherine's death had considerably diminished the possibility of an invasion by Charles V. The long shadow cast over Henry's marriage was surely a thing of the past—Anne was now the only person in England claiming to be queen.

These celebrations were, however, short-lived. On 24 January, just over two weeks after Catherine's death, Henry's horse fell heavily at the jousting tournament. Henry was a large man, and would have been wearing fifty kilos of armour. He was thrown from a horse perhaps seventeen hands high, and, although he was unconscious for two hours, it is remarkable that he did not sustain more serious injuries. Five days later Anne miscarried again. It is not known whether this was a consequence of Henry's accident, but news of it could not have helped. The miscarriage was public knowledge—Anne's collapse had been witnessed.

It was reported that the child was male and miscarried at about fifteen to seventeen weeks. A whole mythology has been built round this baby—in particular, that he was deformed—but it is unlikely that any medical experts were in attendance at the time, and the reports of deformity date back only to many years after the actual event.

The 16th-century mind linked a deformed baby with either sexual misbehaviour by the parents, or the practice of witchcraft. Some subsequent chroniclers used the former idea to endorse the accusations of sexual immorality by Anne that were made later at her trial. The problem here is that there was no mention of a deformed foetus at the trial.

Others believed that Anne must have been a witch and that Henry concurred, so he had to extricate himself from the marriage.[2] Credence has been given to this view because of a report that Henry told Chapuys, the imperial ambassador, that he was seduced into the marriage by 'sortileges' (meaning witchcraft). But this is a second-hand report of a conversation that would have been conducted in French. Which French word did Henry actually use? Did Henry mean 'bewitched', the same word Tyndale used in his 1526 translation of Galatians 3:1, where there is no suggestion of witchcraft? The verse comes to us in the Authorized Version as: 'O foolish Galatians, who hath bewitched you, that ye should not obey the truth, before whose eyes Jesus Christ hath been evidently set forth, crucified among you?'

Both superstitious explanations of the so-called deformed foetus have been repeated by historians in the years since Anne's death, neither having any basis in fact—demonstrating the disservice that history has done to her memory. Despite the miscarriage Anne recovered quickly and comforted her staff, telling them 'it was for the best'.

Nonetheless the miscarriage was a turning point for Anne; it was commented at the time that she had 'miscarried of her saviour'. Undoubtedly it was a key fact in her ultimate demise. The birth of a son would have strengthened her position as queen. She knew she was vulnerable—she had come from a middle-ranking aristocratic family and ascended to the highest position in the land. She did not have the privilege of a royal pedigree: she was not some foreign princess brought from abroad to cement an international alliance but was totally dependent on her relationship with Henry. A son would have insulated her from her enemies. But it was not to be.

So the euphoria after the death of Catherine proved to be short-lived, but what was worse for Anne was that several new scenarios now began to emerge. Since marrying Anne, Henry had been reluctant to accept Mary as a legitimate heir to the throne as this would have meant conceding that his marriage to Catherine was legitimate—and therefore his marriage to Anne, illegitimate. But now that that obstacle had gone there was no reason why he should not declare his first daughter Mary to be a 'child of good faith', and allow Mary as firstborn to become legitimate in law as heir presumptive, making Elizabeth second in line. As we shall see later, there was new pressure on Henry from the conservative faction at court to do this. (Some years after Anne's death, he did. Mary eventually came to the throne, and then on Mary's death, Elizabeth became queen.)

Was Henry now tiring of Anne? Her vivacious wit and sharp mind, her integrity, and her new ideas had been seen by him as a breath of fresh air—but he had risked all for her, and now he stood alone against the power of the Church and the Holy Roman Empire. Anne was creating her own power base in the many appointments she had influenced—particularly in the Church. This began to worry Thomas Cromwell—and possibly Henry himself. A quick wit can soon cross the dividing line to a sharp tongue; it was said that Anne could best Henry in many an argument.

Moreover, the miscarriage had played on Henry's superstitious mind—

God was not blessing his new marriage, so did God not approve of Anne? Jesus in the New Testament specifically denies that adverse acts of providence can be interpreted as God's particular judgement on individuals—but nonetheless Henry's view was typical of the 16th-century mindset.[3] Furthermore, persuading Henry to put aside the love of his life was a difficult task, one that was obviously doomed to failure if it meant he had to take back the old and barren Catherine. But with Catherine's death new possibilities opened up—perhaps Henry could now be tempted with a new, younger, potentially more fertile wife? Such a woman would be innocent of any charge of causing the split with Rome, and so would be accepted by both conservatives and Reformers. Henry could even have his longed-for papal blessing on the match.

Enter Jane Seymour. The contrast with Anne was marked. She is described as fair, younger than Anne by several years; a quiet, gentle, self-effacing woman. It is said she lacked Anne's charisma—certainly no one ever described her as witty.

Chapuys said of her: 'She is of middle height, and nobody thinks that she has much beauty. Her complexion is so whitish that she may be called rather pale. She is a little over twenty-five … not very intelligent and is said to be rather haughty.'[4]

Anne had set the precedent—an English noblewoman (rather than a foreign princess) could aspire to marry the King. And Jane had powerful backers—the Catholic Seymours, seeing their opportunity, had allied themselves with the conservatives at court. Chapuys, the imperial ambassador, was co-opted for help. He readily agreed, having never accepted Anne as a legitimate wife to Henry as she had displaced his emperor's aunt. Jane Seymour was duly coached on how to present herself to Henry, how to work on his fears about the validity of his marriage to Anne—and also remind him, if such was required, of his lack of a son. Further, Jane was taught to play Anne's 'game'—no sexual intercourse without marriage.

Some have seen a kind of poetic justice in this—that Anne was ousted by Jane using the same tactics as she had used. The comparison does not bear examination. Henry's marriage to Catherine was all but over before he even considered Anne. Henry was immediately attracted to her, and pursued her relentlessly. In contrast Jane was dangled before Henry like a carrot on a string. Anne was always clear that it was marriage or nothing; Jane accepted Henry's initial flirtations and only increased her price once the chance of marriage appeared. Anne was her own woman and acted out of principle; Jane was taking instructions from others with an ulterior motive—that of ousting Anne and gaining a crown.

It was at this time that Anne and Thomas Cromwell began to have differences; certainly by 1 April it was known at court that there was a distance between them. One matter of disagreement was that Anne favoured an alliance with the German Protestants, but Cromwell on the death of Catherine saw an opportunity to form an alliance with the Emperor and had secret talks with Chapuys to that end. Another issue was the reform of the monasteries. Cromwell wanted a radical solution—his aim was for the State to confiscate the wealth of as many monasteries as possible, with the result that most would be closed. In order to achieve this a report had been issued cataloguing many of the abuses that the Church had been guilty of allowing, if not actually encouraging.

The parliamentary bill for the dissolution of the monasteries was waiting to be passed. The difference of opinion was about the best way forward; the status quo was not an option. Anne and other prominent Reformers, including John Skip, her almoner (a sort of chaplain), wanted the monastery assets to be used for a better purpose—to be allocated to education and charitable causes. The college at Stoke by Clare was an example of what Anne hoped to achieve (see Chapter 11). Few doubted Cromwell's motives—he wanted to ease Henry's financial constraints and give him a significant fund of money which he could use for royal patronage. The ultimate goal, it appeared to many, was not reform, but theft. Needless to say the bill had Henry's enthusiastic support.

On 2 April, the Sunday before Easter, John Skip preached a sermon at the Chapel Royal at Greenwich which caused considerable consternation—his text was John 8:46 where Jesus is recorded saying, 'Can any of you prove me guilty of sin?' In the congregation were the King and Queen and all the important members of court and Council. Skip developed his sermon so that the 'you' in the text was the congregation, and the 'me' the preacher—or rather, the clergy. So Skip claimed that the congregation, in particular the advisors to the King, were unreasonably targeting all clergy in their moves against the Church. He further hinted at Henry's lax sexual morals with a reference to Solomon's many wives. He then went on to attack Cromwell personally, using the Old Testament book of Esther to make his point.

In the story, Esther, the faithful Jewish woman, became the wife of the Persian ruler Xerxes in order to save her people from persecution. The chief advisor to Xerxes was a man called Haman—he had ordered the massacre of the Jews. The outcome was that Esther's counsel prevailed, the Jews were saved, and Haman was hanged. This story would have been very well known to the congregation; it wouldn't have been difficult for them to work out the code. Henry was Xerxes, the faithful clerics were the Jews, Cromwell was Haman, and of course Queen Anne was Esther.

Skip was even more direct—he changed an element in the well-known Bible story. In the text Haman offered to pay Xerxes 10,000 talents to cover the cost of the archers that would be required to destroy the Jews. In contrast Skip had Haman promise Xerxes that the destruction of the Jews would release 10,000 talents for the royal exchequer—the Jews (the clerics) in effect paying for their own destruction. Skip then had Xerxes telling Haman he could keep some of the money for himself.

This was not a subtle approach to the situation—and few evangelicals today would accept such a method of biblical exegesis. But Anne must have given sanction for this sermon. What drove Anne and Skip to do this? It appears that Anne, and others, had been misled. Documents issued by Cromwell's office were full of 'spin'. They talked in vague terms about the confiscated assets being used 'to the pleasure of Almighty God'. The first warning came when Sawley Abbey in Yorkshire was sold in a private deal by the King to one of his cronies—Sir Arthur Darcy—before the Dissolution Bill was even on the statute book. Anne learned, perhaps too late, that the real intention of Cromwell and Henry was the total secularization of the confiscated assets. Cromwell had always aligned himself with the evangelical reforming group at court, so why was he pursuing this path? What are we to make of him as a Christian? Undoubtedly he was a most able politician, a student of Machiavelli. The New Testament is clear that good works do not save us: 'For it is by grace you have been saved, through faith—and this not from yourselves, it is the gift of God.'[5] But Jesus says that each tree is recognized by its own fruit.[6] In other words, deeds show the true nature of a person. Cromwell now began to reveal himself. His continuing machinations eventually had terrible consequences for many true believers.

Anne sent Hugh Latimer, the country's foremost preacher, into the battle, telling him to address the matter in his next sermon before the King. He preached on Luke 20, in which Jesus tells the parable of the tenants denying rents to the vineyard owner. The point Latimer made was that once these tenants had been evicted the vineyard was not destroyed but handed over to more worthy occupants. The lesson was clear—the monasteries should not be destroyed but rather given over to a better use, to be places of study and charitable works.

It appears that Anne also persuaded Archbishop Cranmer to write to Cromwell about the matter, which he did on 22 April. A delegation of abbots and priors came to see Anne personally, asking for protection from the coming decimation of their property and livings. She took the opportunity to deliver a lecture to them, criticizing the corruption they had overseen and their resistance in the past to evangelical preaching. But she did not leave them without hope when in her closing remarks she said, 'Until such time as you shall cleanse and purify your corrupt life and doctrine, God will not cease to send his plagues upon you to your utter subversion.'[7]

Seizing on this they offered the Queen money to support preachers and scholars of her choice. Latymer says Anne in turn organized a group of men to manage the distribution of these funds. If this is correct Anne was colluding in diverting Church funds to thwart their seizure by the State—something the Dissolution Bill specifically forbade.

Despite Anne's best efforts, however, the Dissolution Bill was duly passed—but it did include a personal veto for the King. In other words, Henry could reprieve any monastery he so chose. Cromwell knew that he would have to battle against Anne's influence with Henry if she appealed to the King to make a special case for any monastery she considered worth saving. It is known that she sought to reprieve the Yorkshire convent of Nun Monkton and possibly also the convent at Catesby. It is suggested that there were many others.

Cromwell now realized that he was caught between a rock and a hard place. Henry was keen on pushing through the dissolution to get the income into the exchequer; Anne was not. If Cromwell agreed with Anne that some should be saved, he antagonized the King; if he supported Henry's aggressive secularization, he antagonized Anne. He must have known how Henry had crumbled when Anne confronted him about Cromwell's former employer Cardinal Wolsey—would he be the next to be despatched?

Meanwhile Cromwell was in secret talks with Chapuys for a renewed alliance with the Emperor. These negotiations were with the King's consent, but, unknown to Henry, Charles V wanted, as part of the deal, Mary's claim to the throne legitimized. Not only was Mary Charles V's cousin, but the Emperor also saw that if Mary eventually acceded to the throne it would cement the relationship between the Empire and England. Cromwell did not think that making Mary heir to the throne was any longer a problem—but this was a misreading of the situation. Henry was furious; he would not be dictated to. The succession of Elizabeth was non-negotiable.

The timing of all this is important in light of the speed of subsequent events—as late as 30 April Henry was holding out against Charles V for recognition by the Emperor of the legitimacy of his marriage to Anne, and of Elizabeth as the rightful heir. Chapuys, who had thought a deal was imminent, realized that Cromwell had badly misread the situation, and went to lick his wounds. Cromwell received a very public rebuke from Henry, who had already cautioned him at the end of 1535 for exceeding his authority. He took to his bed and stayed away from court for a week, claiming to be ill. Cromwell had now been thwarted by Anne both at home and abroad. His alienation from her and the Boleyn faction at court was clear for all to see. Moreover, despite his political gifts he was never really part of the 'in-crowd' at court. He was not particularly well liked—he was considered more as a civil servant: a very useful employee who had mastered the messy bureaucratic machine. But in a day when class distinction was everything, the aristocrats who made up most of the King's close advisors considered that this son of a blacksmith was simply 'not one of us'. He was now completely isolated at court, and had even managed to cross Henry by proposing an imperial alliance with conditions Henry deemed unacceptable. Was history repeating itself? Cardinal Wolsey, despite years of service to the King at home, had also stumbled in the arena of foreign policy.

Cromwell had to find a way forward. He had achieved much with Anne's patronage and she in turn had benefited from his political skills. But he realized he could never get past Anne, and while she was queen he would always be one step removed from Henry—the source of all real power. So this complex, clever man made a sinister and shocking decision: to switch his support to the Seymours, get rid of Anne, and see a pliable Jane as queen.

He still believed that he could count on Henry's support—but only if he could execute a plan quickly and deliver Henry a new queen. Why? Because Henry still had no confidence in a female succession; he was forty-five and it was becoming less and less likely, as far as he could see, that Anne was going to give him the required male heir, leaving on his death a divided kingdom—those who backed Mary against those who backed Elizabeth. The potential for a civil war was great and—even worse—for a possible intervention from the Emperor and the Pope to remove Elizabeth and marry Mary off to a foreign prince, leaving England as a colony of the Holy Roman Empire.

Nonetheless the task Cromwell set himself was complex and full of risk. He did not want to see the return of the monasteries to the Church—or the Church resume its old position in English life. He was for reform in as much as he wanted to see the modern split between Church and State, and the Church very much in its own (small) corner. So he had to run with the conservatives in court, and support the Catholic faction in order to depose Anne, then do a volte-face, turn against his new friends, and continue to pursue the reform agenda. Such a plan would have defeated anybody but a gifted student of Machiavelli and a political genius. Cromwell was both.

Notes

1 Tradition hostile to Anne has Henry weeping with grief and Anne as the one dressed in bright yellow, but neither is true. See **Starkey,** *Six wives: the queens of Henry VIII,* p. 550.

2   Warnicke, in her biography of Anne published in 1998, takes this view—that accusations of witchcraft were at the root of Anne's fall.

3   For example, Luke 13:1–5 and John 9:1–3.

4   Quoted by **Ives,** *The Life and Death of Anne Boleyn*, p. 302.

5   Ephesians 2:8.

6   Luke 6:44.

7   Quoted by **Ives,** *The Life and Death of Anne Boleyn*, p. 311.

A faith in action

B efore relating Anne's dreadful demise it is useful to consider what mark she had made on English national life in the fifteen years since her return from the French court: first as a debutante, then as unofficial fiancée of the King, and finally as Queen of England. Anne displayed two clear motivations in her years as queen—to provide a son for Henry and so secure the succession, and to promote biblical Christianity by disseminating the Bible's teachings. The hoped-for-son never came; it cost her her life. But it can be shown that she pursued with vigour, and some success, the cause of the gospel during her time of influence at the Tudor court.

A personal testimony

Personal Bible study was Anne's practice; her chaplain Latymer said that 'Her highness was very expert in the French tongue, exercising herself continually in reading the French Bible and other French books of like effect and conceived great pleasure in the same, wherefore her highness charged her chaplains to be furnished of all kind of French books that reverently treated of the holy scripture.'[1]

Louis de Brun, in a work dedicated to Anne, in 1531 wrote of her:

When I consider the great affection and real passion which you have for the French tongue, I am not surprised that you are never found, if circumstances permit, without your having some book in French in your hand which is of use and value in pointing out and finding the true and narrow way to all virtues, as, for example, translations of the Holy Scriptures, reliable and full of sound doctrines ... And most of all ... I have seen you continually reading those helpful letters of St Paul which contain all the fashion and rule to live righteously, in every good manner of behaviour, which you know well and practise, thanks to your continual reading of them.[2]

It is in these Pauline letters that Anne would have read the great statements about faith, including:

Therefore no one will be declared righteous in his sight by observing the law; rather, through the law we become conscious of sin. But now a righteousness from God, apart from law, has been made known, to which the Law and the Prophets testify. This righteousness from God comes through faith in Jesus Christ to all who believe. There is no difference, for all have sinned and fall short of the glory of God, and are justified freely by his grace through the redemption that came by Christ Jesus.[3]

This faith, Galatians tells us, 'expresses itself through love'.[4]

Starkey says: '[Anne] continued this practice of conspicuous piety throughout the days of her prosperity, reading improving works herself and encouraging her ladies to read them as well.'[5]

Anne's doctrinal position

Anne, her brother George, and her father were all described as Lutherans—but this does not mean they held a clear doctrinal position that would identify them with everything that Luther said. Nor was there any direct connection with Wycliffe and the Lollards of an earlier time. The thing that united them was an absolute conviction of the importance of the Bible—in other words, they were evangelicals. The Roman Catholic Church was itself in a state of flux. Many within the Church, on reading the New Testament for themselves, alongside the new books coming from Europe, had begun to see that the doctrinal position of the Roman Church bore little relationship to Scripture. Some embraced the 'new learning' wholeheartedly, some did in part. For others their journey to faith was a slow one, with doubts resurfacing on the way. Thomas Bilney (see below) and Archbishop Cranmer embraced the 'new learning', then shrank back in horror at the thought of their ruined careers, the damage to others it would cause, and the very real prospect of their own torture and burning. Then later they received renewed strength and witnessed to the Saviour, going to their violent deaths with enormous courage and heroism. These heroes of faith faltered—but who would be so bold as to pass judgement on them? Today we are surrounded by considered doctrinal statements that were hammered out over the hundred or so years after these tumultuous events, secure in the knowledge that the evangelical cause largely triumphed—a perspective denied them.

Anne was the catalyst in the break with Rome

Without Anne it is almost certain that Henry would not have made the break from Rome. Not only did she provide the motivation, she also gave him the scriptural arguments to strengthen his resolve. Anne brought evangelical books directly to Henry, marking particular passages for his attention and discussion. Henry took his religion seriously. As has been seen he had made an international reputation for himself in his *Assertion of the Seven Sacraments*, published in 1521, attacking Martin Luther and his teachings. It is unlikely that Henry wrote the work unaided, but over his life he built a library of more than a thousand theological books. There was correspondence between Henry and Sir James Boleyn (Anne's uncle), defending a more conservative line, and Hugh Latimer and Nicholas Shaxton (both appointed bishops in 1535), who adopted more evangelical views. Henry was knowledgeable about the theological issues of his time—although there is no evidence that he embraced a personal faith in Christ. Henry's keen personal interest in theology was not that unusual, but accepting lively debate when the leading protagonist was a woman, indeed his own wife, was. The Bible, not just church and 'religion', was the frequent dinner conversation in the Boleyn home, and Anne took the habit to the King's own dining table. William Latymer says that Anne and Henry never dined 'without some argument of Scripture thoroughly debated'.[6]

Key figures could count on Anne's support

Anne's influence did not stop with Henry: the Archbishop of Canterbury was a known supporter of Anne, the Lord Privy Seal was her father, and the King's secretary was Thomas Cromwell, also firmly in the Boleyn camp, or at least, so it was thought; the Lord Chancellor, Thomas Audley, was also on very favourable terms with her. There was a circle of friends at court who were sympathetic to reform and would obviously be emboldened when Anne was crowned queen.

Anne pressured Henry to protect evangelicals at home

Anne's influence in theological matters had already displayed itself well before her marriage. In 1528 she had written to Cardinal Wolsey to 'remember the parson of Honey Lane for my sake'. All Hallows, Honey

Lane, near Cheapside in the City of London, was a centre for evangelicals attracting great numbers to hear the preachers. The rector, Dr Robert Forman, and his curate, Thomas Garrett, were under investigation for heresy. Garrett particularly was involved in importing books that were more radical than any which Anne's agents handled. It was a brave move by Anne to write to the Cardinal, because Wolsey prided himself in tracking down the trade in books and prosecuting those involved, boasting to Pope Clement VII about his efforts. Anne also persuaded Henry to get Wolsey to intervene on behalf of the Prior of Reading, John Shirburn, who in 1529 had been arrested for possessing Lutheran books sent to him by Garrett. That Henry should intervene on behalf of an acknowledged Lutheran when he himself was still a staunch advocate of Catholic doctrine shows the remarkable extent of Anne's influence.

The medical doctor William Butts who had cared for Anne when she had the 'sweat' was an unofficial talent-spotter for her. He was in trouble in 1528 over the circulation of prohibited books at Oxford University, along with Thomas Bilney, Hugh Latimer, and Matthew Parker (who later became Anne's private chaplain); Anne had to intercede with Cardinal Wolsey to protect them from the consequences of dealing in evangelical books. These men had convincing personal testimonies. Thomas Bilney, on reading the New Testament published by Erasmus in 1516, said, 'I felt a marvellous comfort and quietness'. Latimer in turn said of Bilney: 'By his confession I learned more than in twenty years before'. On 19 August 1531 Bilney was burnt at the stake for preaching Reformed doctrine. In October 1555 it was Latimer's turn, when he was burnt at the stake outside Balliol College, Oxford.

Thomas Alway, prosecuted by Wolsey for having banned books, wrote to Anne: 'I remembered how many deeds of pity your goodness has done within these few years … without respect of any persons, as well as to strangers and aliens as to many of this land, as well to poor as to the rich.'[7]

Anne pressured Henry to protect evangelicals abroad

Anne also personally intervened to help evangelicals in trouble in mainland Europe. When Francis I turned against the Reformers in France Anne did her best to help them, including Nicholas Bourbon, a poet prominent among the evangelicals of the 1520s. His patroness was Anne's friend Marguerite, sister of Francis I. Bourbon was arrested but managed to get a letter out of prison to Dr William Butts, who informed Anne. Henry duly intervened in France on the poet's behalf. Bourbon came to England, lodging with the doctor at Anne's expense. His writings show that he soon became part of the English evangelical scene. He wrote of Anne: 'How can I express my thanks, still less, Oh Queen repay you? I confess I have not the resources. But the Spirit of Jesus which enflames you wholly with his fire, he has the wherewithal to give you your due.'[8]

A book that had caused particular controversy was Simon Fish's *A Supplication for Beggars*—a supplication being a petition, and the beggars being ordinary English people who were described as being bled dry by the money and lands that went to the Church. The book urged emancipation from Rome's control, and Thomas More was recruited to write a rebuttal. Fish had to flee abroad, but Henry offered immunity to him and his wife. They eventually returned to England and Fish discussed his work personally with the King.

Soon after her coronation Anne worked to restore the Antwerp merchant Richard Herman to membership of the Society of Merchants from which he had been expelled for helping to distribute copies of the New Testament in English. In May 1535 William Tyndale was arrested in Antwerp, betrayed by one of Thomas More's agents. Anne acted with Cromwell in putting pressure on Henry, who had the necessary letters written in an attempt to secure his release. For whatever reason this was unsuccessful, the famous Bible translator eventually being strangled and then burnt on 6 October 1536.

Anne influenced key Church appointments

Anne worked hard to ensure that key Church appointments went to evangelicals, and her influence predated her coronation; she was recorded as far back as 1528 putting pressure on Cardinal Wolsey to appoint clerics who would promote reform. Before 1532 newly appointed bishops were mainly of orthodox Catholic persuasion; from 1532 to 1536 eleven bishops were appointed, nine of whom were considered to be evangelicals, such as Thomas Cranmer, Hugh Latimer, Nicholas Shaxton, Thomas Goodrich, and (although taking up office after her death) John Skip. On her death there was a shift back to orthodox Catholic appointments—out of the twenty-one men nominated in the ten years after Anne's fall only two can be considered to be evangelicals: Holbeach and Ferrar.[9] And it wasn't just bishops: wherever possible she took a personal interest in endeavouring to secure the appointment of evangelical clergy further down the hierarchy. Anne was allowed to choose her own chaplains, and she chose well—usually from young Reformist scholars at Cambridge. She was particularly keen on Matthew Parker. Her secretary wrote two letters in one day urging him to come at once—and not to bother with too much luggage! He was soon Dean at the church of Stoke by Clare in Suffolk, which had a college of priests attached to it—known as a 'collegiate' church. Just before her death she asked Parker to take care of her daughter Elizabeth. He became Elizabeth's first Archbishop of Canterbury.

Anne saw the Bible in English as a goal

Anne's fluency in French gave her the privileged position of reading the Bible for herself—a privilege she was keen to see extended to all her English-speaking subjects. According to Latymer she kept a Bible in English in her rooms for anyone to read who wished to do so; if this was the whole Bible it must have been towards the end of her life, since Coverdale's Bible (printed in Zurich) did not appear until 1535. Latymer might have been referring to the 1534 copy of Tyndale's New Testament, which it is known Anne owned and treasured, and kept on display at court despite it being a banned book in England.

Anne promoted the trade in Bibles and evangelical books

This trade was illegal. Her brother George was particularly active in the trade; with the protection of his family connections he would smuggle controversial works back to England in his diplomatic bag. Many were by Lefèvre and included *The Epistles and Gospels for the Fifty-two Weeks of the Year*—the 16th-century equivalent of today's devotional daily readings. The printer and publisher was Simon du Bois who eventually had to seek refuge with Marguerite—Anne's old mentor. As recently as 1998 it was established that George translated the French commentary into

English. It carried a dedication to Anne showing a strong affection between brother and sister, and a common cause—the evangelical faith. Another work was the text of the Bible book Ecclesiastes with a commentary, also probably by George, emphasizing in clear vivid language the need for a living faith in Christ. This gives credence to the account of George's speech on the scaffold as he faced the executioner's axe, which has him saying:

Truly so that the Word should be among the people of the realm I took upon myself great labour to urge the king to permit the printing of the Scriptures to go unimpeded among the commons of the realm in their own language. And truly to God I was one of those who did most to procure the matter to place the Word of God among the people because of the love and affection which I bear for the gospel and the truth of Christ's words.[10]

It was not just through George that Anne worked—she had her own contacts abroad, especially in Antwerp. Agents there supplied her with evangelical books, and she in turn supported those involved in the trade. Among the Reformers in Antwerp was William Tyndale; his translation of the New Testament was being smuggled into England in considerable numbers.

The Church authorities tried to get rid of his New Testament wherever possible. The Bishop of London publicly burned copies, even buying copies abroad in order to destroy them, and recruited Thomas More to write tracts against Tyndale's writings.

Anne's silkwomen at court included evangelicals who were involved in importing illegal Bibles. Rose Hickman, a daughter of one of the silk suppliers, recalled her father saying that 'Queen Anne Boleyn ... caused him to get her the gospels and epistles written in parchment in French together with the psalms'.[11]

Anne was keen to see the monasteries reformed, not dissolved

Anne's concern for the monastic houses is well documented. In 1533 she persuaded Cromwell to investigate conditions at Thetford Priory and also asked him about the Abbey of Vale Royal in Cheshire. She was fully behind the campaign to impose new conditions which Cromwell began to put into effect in the summer of 1535—including discouraging the display of relics and the claiming of false miracles. One such relic was at Hailes Abbey; they loved to display what they claimed was a specimen of the actual blood that Christ shed at Calvary, blood that had never congealed. Many believed that the mere sight of it would give them grace. It is recorded that Anne registered her disapproval—but the relic was not removed until after her death, when it was exposed as a fraud.

But Anne's emphasis with the monasteries was on reform, not dissolution. Furthermore, like many, she did not see the 'new learning' as necessitating a break with Rome; many hoped to see the old Church reformed. John Skip, Anne's chaplain, in that same controversial sermon of 2 April 1536, when he preached on the (altered) story of Esther, had defended the ceremonies of the Church—including the holy water and holy bread—saying that surely no one wanted them abandoned; they had no objective sacred power but were rather aids to memory.[12] Skip showed that he considered Henry's reform of the Church to be legitimate, by referring to the Old Testament story of Moses in the wilderness. When the Israelites were being attacked by snakes, on God's instructions Moses held up a brass snake on a pole; all those who looked on it 'would live', a symbol of the future Christ.[13] The brass snake became an object of worship when subsequently mounted on the temple wall. Skip pointed out that it was the new King Hezekiah who took the image and smashed it in pieces—a clear inference being that Henry's legitimate role was to restrain the Church in any corrupt practice. Skip could not have preached the sermon without Anne's approval.

Anne was concerned about education

Anne was known to be generous in her financial support of students, even promising help to Thomas Winter, Cardinal Wolsey's illegitimate son. In addition she made financial contributions to Oxford and Cambridge Universities. She financially supported Matthew Parker's work at the collegiate church of Stoke by Clare, where he established regular preaching, a lecturer on the Bible to teach four days a week, and a new grammar school with fee-paying and free places, Anne being named the new founder.

A practical religion

Anne made it clear at the beginning of her reign that her religion was one that was to have a practical outworking. She told her new household that it was to be run on the grounds of equity, justice, and value for money. Staff were to attend chapel daily—but also keep away from the brothels and other places of ill repute.

She was particularly concerned about the poor, and set an example for others when the Royal Maundy money was substantially increased. The ladies of her household worked sewing clothes in the winter which were then taken on progress in the summer and distributed to the poor under the supervision of the local priest and two parishioners. Individual cases of poverty would be reported to her via her chaplains. An example is the story of one of Hugh Latimer's parishioners, who lost most of his cattle; when Anne arrived in the parish she interviewed the man's wife and gave her the substantial gift of £20. John Foxe, in his *Acts and Monuments*, talks much of Anne's charity and suggests that she gave as much as £15,000 in one year in poor relief. This is probably an error of transmission—a figure of £1,500 pounds is more likely; even then it is still a very substantial sum indeed.

Anne sought to influence Parliament on behalf of the poor

It was not just at a personal level that Anne took action: it is difficult not to see her influence in the legislation passed in 1536, when Parliament dealt radically to tackle the widespread poverty in the country. It was drafted in part by William Marshall, who had studied poverty in France and how it was tackled in Ypres, the resulting report being dedicated to Anne. Henry attended Parliament in person to endorse the new legislation and promised to contribute to the cost of its implementation

In the opinion of others ...

John Foxe, writing in the 16th century, recorded: 'What a zealous defender she was of Christ's gospel all the world doth know, and her acts do and will declare to the world's end.[14]

Alexander Ales wrote in a letter to Elizabeth I that 'True religion in England had its commencement and its end with your mother.'[15]

And in our own day, Joanna Denny writes: 'Anne Boleyn was the catalyst for the Reformation, the initiator of the Protestant religion in England.'[16]

Richard Rex: 'The alliance between crown and Reformers forged during the divorce controversy was decisive for the survival of the evangelical movement.'[17]

Professor Eric Ives, the foremost academic expert on Boleyn: 'Anne Boleyn was not a catalyst in the English Reformation; she was a key element in the equation … a thousand days of support for reform from the throne itself. And hindsight can say more. The breach in the dyke of tradition which she encouraged and protected made the flood first of reformed, and later of more specifically Protestant Christianity, unstoppable.'[18]

Notes

1 **Ives,** *The Life and Death of Anne Boleyn,* p. 268.

2 Ibid. p. 269.

3 Romans 3:20–24.

4 Galatians 5:6.

5 **Starkey,** *Six wives: the queens of Henry VIII,* p. 369.

6 **Denny,** p. 210.

7 Ibid. p. 128.

8 Quoted by **Ives,** *The Life and Death of Anne Boleyn,* p. 275.

9 **Rex,** pp. 143–145; **Ives,** *The Life and Death of Anne Boleyn,* p. 261.

10 **Ives,** *The Life and Death of Anne Boleyn,* p. 272.

11 **Denny,** p. 212.

12 **Ives,** 'Anne Boleyn and the Early Reformation in England', *Historical Journal,* p. 395.

13 Numbers 21:4-9; 2 Kings 18:4; John 3:14–15.

14 **John Foxe,** *Acts and Monuments,* v. 175.

15 Letter to Queen Elizabeth, 1 September 1559. Quoted in **Ives,** *The Life and Death of Anne Boleyn,* p. 264.

16 **Denny,** p. 132.

17 **Rex,** p. 167.

18 **Ives,** *The Life and Death of Anne Boleyn,* pp. 260–261.

The coup

The exact sequence of events leading up to the first execution of a queen in English history, and what lay behind them, has been the subject of debate by many historians. But what is certain is that sometime early in 1536 Cromwell had it in mind to move against Anne—and when he eventually did it was with ruthless, cold efficiency. By the end of May Anne, her brother George, and several others, were dead. How did this happen? Henry and Anne even at Easter had seemed as inseparable as ever. Cromwell realized that drastic action was required. The only way of getting rid of Anne that anybody could think of—showing that Henry's marriage to her was null because of the earlier 'pre-contract' she had with Henry Percy—had been tried before, but it was a non-runner. Percy was prepared to swear on any oath that no such pre-contract existed.

On 24 April Nicolas Carew was created by Henry one of the prestigious Knights of the Garter. Anne had hoped that her brother George would have been the one to be honoured. This was a clear signal to Cromwell that the tide was turning in his favour, and he decided to go ahead with his new plan—a fantastic course of action. He would accuse the Queen, and others he wanted brought down, of adultery and treason. Did he have the King's explicit, or even tacit, agreement? It is not known. Cromwell needed a commission of 'oyer and terminer' (to hear and determine) to investigate the charges—and for the final repudiation of Anne, the recall of Parliament. On the same day as Carew got his knighthood the required commission was set up (seemingly without the King's signature) with a general remit to investigate and try offences for treason. On 27 April writs were sent out to summon Parliament; this had to have Henry's agreement, but Cromwell may have placated Henry with some excuse for its recall. Even if the King was not in Cromwell's confidence, the new Knight of the Garter Nicolas Carew was, as were almost certainly the Seymours, who were keen to see Jane as Anne's replacement.

Cromwell had laid his trap, and now he was waiting for somebody to step into it. What was he hoping for? Cromwell knew that Anne was a lively, friendly person who ran her household in a much less formal way than her predecessor Catherine; she was interested in the people around her and enjoyed light-hearted banter. The court was full of ambitious, attractive young men and women with time on their hands. Cromwell realized that in this heady environment, which Anne had failed to check as perhaps she should, an exchange could easily be twisted by him into something else; all he had to do was wait.

Late on Saturday 29 April, or early the next day, Anne and Sir Henry Norris, the 'groom of the stool', argued.[1] Anne accused Norris, a widower ten years older then her, of having inappropriate feelings towards her. The King got to know about this, and, although all seems to have been sorted out by Sunday evening, as is suggested by Sir Henry joining in the revelry of the May Day jousts the next day, the King nonetheless postponed for a week a trip to Calais that had been planned for some time.

That same Saturday there was a minor altercation between Anne and Mark Smeaton, a young and lowly court musician. The story reached Cromwell, who the next day had him brought to his house. After twenty-four hours of interrogation Smeaton confessed to adultery with the Queen and was committed to the Tower, arriving at about 6 o'clock on the Monday afternoon. How this confession was obtained is not known. Certainly pressure, if not actual torture, would have been brought to bear, and probably he was promised imprisonment or a quick death if he confessed, rather than the agony of being dragged through the streets half strangled, then castrated and disembowelled—all while still conscious.

Now Cromwell had a confession from a minor musician and the possibility of taking out the Queen and Henry Norris, one of the King's most trusted advisors. But his real target was the whole Boleyn faction, so he had to keep up the momentum. He left the King with Sir Nicholas Carew and the Seymours, who duly worked on his emotions. Henry VIII fell into the trap, and with his amazing capacity for self-pity imagined he had been wronged, even believing that Anne had taken a hundred lovers. He saw himself as the victim of a great tragedy, later carrying round in his pocket his version of events for others to read and so not miss any detail of how he had been duped. The Seymours had done their job well over the preceding months. Henry lapped up his role as a victim, while Jane was dangled before him as his prize.

Despite these events of Saturday 29 and Sunday 30 April, the May Day tournaments on the Monday went ahead as if nothing was happening. The King seemed in good spirits; all his old friends were there—including Anne's brother George, and Sir Henry Norris. The King, however, did not take part and when handed a note left rather abruptly for Whitehall, travelling on horseback with just six others, including Norris. The King never saw Anne again. On the journey Norris was questioned repeatedly by Henry about his alleged adultery with the Queen. Norris protested his innocence, but was sent to the Tower at dawn on Tuesday 2 May. Anne herself knew nothing of all this—on the morning of that Tuesday she was watching a game of tennis when her uncle the Duke of Norfolk and Cromwell arrived with others. She was arrested and taken to the Tower by boat along the river Thames. Despite attracting the attention of passing river traffic and many onlookers from the riverbanks, Anne managed to keep her composure on this daylight journey from Greenwich. Less than three years had passed since the glittering coronation pageant on the same stretch of river—then as now it had been a fine day. She arrived at the Tower and went in through the Court Gate, never to leave. This time Henry was not there to greet her with a kiss: instead, waiting for her was Sir William Kingston, the Lieutenant of the Tower, but not, as she had thought, to show her to a dungeon; rather he said that she was to stay in the royal apartments. Anne's relief then overwhelmed her, and she went into some sort of nervous collapse.

She appeared to rehearse out loud all the things that could possibly have led to such a terrible misunderstanding. She related the story of the quarrel with Henry Norris. Apparently she had asked Norris why he was postponing his proposed marriage to Margaret (Madge) Shelton, to which he gave a non-committal reply. Anne unwisely said: 'You look for dead man's shoes; for if ought came to the King but good you would look to have me.' In other words, if the King died, Norris would want to marry her. Anne was an expert at this courtly flirtation, and it was a tradition at court that any gentleman should love the sovereign's wife—but this had gone too far. Norris replied 'that if he thought that he would his head were off'. Anne did not let it drop at that—which led to the quarrel. Furthermore, Anne's specific comments could make it look as though she had a personal interest in Norris, and, more crucially, in the King's demise. But all this conversation had been held in front of others in Anne's household, so it is inconceivable that Anne had been serious about her comments.

Anne then went on to relate another exchange. More than a year earlier she had tackled Francis Weston for neglecting his own wife and flirting with Madge Shelton, the fiancée of Norris. He had replied that he thought Norris was more interested in Anne herself than his intended bride, and went on to say that he himself loved someone better than either his wife or Madge. Anne asked, 'Who is that?' He replied it was Anne herself. Anne related that she 'defiled him'—in other words, told him to be quiet.

Kingston was in Cromwell's pay and was noting all Anne said. This last comment was a gift to Cromwell. He was keen that his grand scheme should not be recognized for what it actually was—a cull of the Boleyn faction at court. Weston was in the camp opposed to the Boleyns—the perfect cover. Weston was immediately arrested—at about the same time as William Brereton, a Boleyn sympathizer.

It is not difficult to explain Anne's emotional state: the suddenness of the arrest; the fantastic, untrue, and totally unexpected charges; the alarming danger of her personal situation and that of the others accused with her. It further must be remembered that it was only three months since her miscarriage and the psychological hurt and hormonal imbalance that that might have caused.

Kingston's next letter to Cromwell gave him ammunition against Mark Smeaton. Anne related what had happened in the exchange the previous Saturday. Anne had asked Smeaton why he looked so sad. Smeaton replied, 'It was no matter' and sighed. It was not a suitable reply for a servant to give a queen: he was suggesting that he too was in love with Anne. Anne retorted: 'You may not look to have me speak to you as I should do to a noble man because you are an inferior person.' This conversation shows Anne keeping her distance from a junior person at court while at the same time expressing a personal concern; nonetheless it was used against her.

Cromwell went next for Anne's brother George. He had tried to reach the King—but Henry was kept well out of the way by Cromwell. George was eventually detained at Whitehall on Tuesday 2 May and transferred to the Tower later that same day. Sir Richard Page and Sir Thomas Wyatt followed on the 8th (although these last two escaped execution). Archbishop Cranmer was similarly kept away from Henry, and had to resort to defending Anne by means of a letter, wanting to plead her innocence while at the same time not wanting (or daring) to criticize the King or his actions: 'I am in such a perplexity, that my mind is clearly amazed; for I never had better opinion in woman, than I had in her; which maketh me to think, that she should not be culpable.'[2]

George Boleyn's own wife, Jane, turned against George and Anne, feeding the King with unsubstantiated stories to support the charges. Jane was executed in 1542 for colluding with Culpeper and Catherine Howard (Henry's fifth wife) in their adulterous relationship. It is said that Jane declared her own death to be God's just punishment on her for the false accusations she had made against George and Anne.

Cromwell did not think that Anne would say anything that would compromise her position; after all, he knew the charges were fabricated. His original instructions to Kingston therefore were to discourage conversation with Anne. So these reports from the Tower of Anne's ramblings, induced by her state of nervous shock, were an undreamed-of bonus for him. Things were falling into place for him in a remarkable way.

But there was still a long way to go. There would have to be two distinct trials. The commoners had to appear before the commission of oyer and terminer sitting in Westminster Hall with a jury. But Anne and her brother were peers and had to be tried by a special tribunal—the court of the Lord High Steward, which was made up of a panel of peers presided over by the Steward, who on this occasion was to be none other than Anne's uncle the Duke of Norfolk.

Despite these correct legal procedures, Anne knew that her days were numbered. When Anne was first taken into custody by Kingston she asked, 'Master Kingston, shall I die without justice?' He replied, 'The poorest subject of the King hath justice.' 'And wherewith she laughed.'[3]

Anne had seen plenty of Tudor justice in her short time as queen.

Notes

1 The groom of the stool was to attend to the King's personal toilet—somewhat remarkably, this was considered to be an honoured and important post.

2 **Denny,** p. 279.

3 Quoted by **Denny,** p. 277.

The trial and execution

O n Tuesday 9 May steps were taken to assemble the grand jury of forty-eight men to hear the charges against the commoners. It had obviously been pre-arranged by Cromwell, as all the relevant people turned up the very next day at Westminster Hall. Because of the seriousness of the charges the jury had little choice but to send the defendants for trial; but to make doubly sure of the outcome Thomas More's son-in-law Giles Heron was appointed jury foreman—many had seen More's execution as Anne Boleyn's doing. Just three short years previously Anne had sat in Westminster Hall resplendent as the new queen—now there was a very different scene. In place of all the paraphernalia of a great banquet was the timber scaffolding of the law courts—the blade of the execution axe turned away from the defendants, to be swung round to face them if a guilty verdict was announced.

On Friday, 12 May 1536 Weston, Brereton, Smeaton and Norris were brought to the Hall. If they had ever doubted the outcome, they did not do so when the trial jury came in. Among the members was the foreman, Edward Willoughby, who owed money to Brereton (Brereton's death would extinguish the debt); Giles Alington, married to Thomas More's stepdaughter, William Askew, a good friend of Henry's daughter Mary; Walter Hungerford, a homosexual and therefore totally dependant on Cromwell's discretion; Robert Dormer, who had opposed the split with Rome; Richard Tempest, although a conservative, firmly in Cromwell's camp; and Thomas Palmer, a gambling friend of the King's.

It is not known whether the make-up of the jury members was challenged—or even whether those who were charged had the right to do so. But they knew the reality of the situation—they had spent their lives at court: there were hundreds directly dependant on royal patronage who would be prepared to 'do their duty' for the King. The defendants' only hope, and a faint one at that, was if the King changed his mind.

Smeaton duly confessed to adultery but pleaded not guilty to the rest of the charges. Norris, Weston, and Brereton pleaded not guilty to all charges. None of them had had any advance warning of the evidence; no defence counsel was allowed. The Crown prosecutors simply interrogated them in open court with the sole aim of securing a verdict. Even the imperial ambassador Chapuys, who wanted so much to see the Boleyn faction destroyed, said it was all based 'upon presumption and certain indications, without valid proof or confession'.[1] There was no surprise when the verdict came—guilty. The axe blade was duly turned towards the defendants; they returned to the Tower to await being hung, drawn, and quartered.

Anne and her brother George had to wait over the weekend as their trial wasn't until Monday 15 May. This was to be in the King's Hall in the Tower. Stands to hold 2,000 spectators were built for the occasion and were still there more than 200 years later. There was a jury of twenty-six peers of the realm, including Henry Percy, who had been so much in love with Anne but was required by the King to be in attendance. Anne was brought in, she sat in the chair, raised her right hand, and pleaded not guilty.

She was now in control of herself and answered effectively, with quiet dignity, dominating the court. She gave a clear 'no' to each of the charges. She had not been unfaithful, she did not promise to marry Norris, she did not hope for the King's death, she had not poisoned Catherine, and she had never planned to poison Mary. She had given some money to Francis Weston—but she had done the same for other young courtiers.

An unsympathetic eyewitness at the time said: 'She made so wise and discreet answers to all things laid against her, excusing herself with her words so clearly as though she had never been faulty to the same.'[2]

Again, even Chapuys said: 'These things she totally denied. And gave a plausible answer to each.'[3]

Each jury member gave his or her verdict, starting at the youngest. They all proclaimed 'guilty'. Anne's uncle pronounced the sentence:

Because thou has offended our sovereign the King's grace in committing treason against his person and here attainted of the same, the law of the realm is this, that thou hast deserved death, and thy judgment is this: that thou shalt be burned here within the Tower of London, on the Green, else to have thy head smitten off, as the King's pleasure shall be further known of the same.[4]

Henry Percy collapsed and had to be helped to his feet. While the presiding Duke of Norfolk's tears could be observed by the onlookers, they could only guess what his true feelings were. He had always seen Anne's marriage as a means to enhance his personal power and wealth. But instead of fulfilling the stereotype of the day, Anne had proved to be an independent, articulate, well-read woman who was prepared to stand her ground for her new-found faith. She had been instrumental in causing the break with Rome, so threatening the status quo of medieval society that had given her uncle so much.

Anne was led from the court and it was now George's turn for the charade. He was charged with high treason and incest against the Queen. Again the plea was not guilty, but George showed himself to be a true Boleyn. His wit and clarity flattened the case against him. One of the charges was that he had impugned the King's virility. When shown a piece of paper and asked if he was guilty of saying what was written, George shocked the court and turned the tables by reading out what Cromwell had wanted kept secret—a comment about the King's supposed sexual inadequacies. Chapuys thought that George performed so well it was 10–1 that he would be acquitted.

On receiving the inevitable guilty verdict George commented that every man was a sinner and that therefore all deserved death. Then he showed his compassion in expressing concern for those to whom he owed money; if the King seized his property it was doubtful any would be paid. Chapuys records that he actually read out a list of his creditors before leaving court. The fate of these troubled George—seemingly more than the terrible end that awaited him.

The approach of death causes even a cynical and hardened 21st-century atheist to consider his or her uncertain future. This focusing of the mind was greatly magnified in the 16th century, with its startling ever-present visual images of the after-life to ponder. Now was time for confessions of any wrongdoing. Nothing was to be gained by holding out against the truth. Those convicted of adultery had the next day or so to reconsider their claim to innocence in the courtroom, when there had perhaps been at least a faint hope of acquittal. But they did not confess. Brereton would not budge, nor would Norris.

There still survive today inscriptions carved into the walls of the Tower cells by the victims—in the Martin Tower the word 'boullen' is scratched into the stonework, and in the Beauchamp Tower, in one of the cells where the men were imprisoned, is a carving of Anne Boleyn's shield of arms, a symbol of a falcon. Ives says:

Which of her 'lovers' made it we do not know, but the image is unmistakable. The tree-stump is there—the barren Henry—the Tudor rose-bush bursting into life, the perching bird whose touch wrought the miracle. But there is one change to the badge which Anne had proudly flourished in the face of the world. This falcon is no longer a royal bird. It has no crown, no sceptre; it stands bareheaded, as did Anne in those last moments on Tower Green.[5]

In the King's great benevolence they were all to be spared the hanging, drawing, and quartering, and instead go straight to the beheading. The men, including George Boleyn, were executed on Wednesday 17 May on Tower Hill. Scaffold speeches in the 1500s had their conventions, rather like the Oscar acceptance speeches of our own day. The executioner's victim was supposed to say how much he or she was a sinner, and that, specifically, he or she deserved death for the crimes committed. While confessing to be a sinner George never admitted to the crimes even in his scaffold speech. Only the young Smeaton said: 'Masters I pray you all pray for me for I have deserved the death.'[6]

Norris said virtually nothing. Weston said, 'I had thought to have lived in abomination yet this twenty or thirty years and then to have made amends.' Brereton said, 'I have deserved to die if it were a thousand deaths. But the cause whereof I die, judge not. But if ye judge, judge the best.' An onlooker said, 'By my troth if any of them were innocent it was he. For either he was innocent or else he died worst of all.'[7]

Each man took his turn to kneel at the scaffold and placed his neck on the block. The axe was swung, the head severed, and the bodies quickly taken away on a cart.

Were they guilty? In the different trials a total of ninety-five jury members had said so. Surely the evidence must have been overwhelming, the verdict and sentence justified?

It is a curious legal point that adultery with the Queen did not carry the death penalty—but treason did. So the prosecution used a novel phrase that her lovers had 'treasonably violated the Queen'. They carefully avoided talk of rape, because they wanted to find Anne herself guilty of consensual adultery. In 1542 legislation was passed making such adultery a statutory treasonable offence—clearly demonstrating that in the 1530s it was not. On this technical point alone the trial was flawed.

Further, the Crown prosecution had a list of dates, places, and accomplices to support the charges of Anne's adulteries, three quarters of which, even after an interval of nearly 500 years, can be shown to be false. In most cases, either Anne was elsewhere, or the co-accused was. There were only two offences for which Anne could not have produced a cast-iron alibi. This betrays the level of cynicism Cromwell had for Tudor justice. In drawing up charges the prosecution did not even bother to check where Anne was, or her alleged lovers. Dates and places for other lesser charges, for example, corrupting men's allegiance with gifts, can similarly, even at this distance, be disproved.

The charge against the defendants that was to be the *coup de grâce* was conspiracy to secure the King's death. The allegation was that the accused met to this end at Westminster on 30 October 1535 and at Greenwich on 8 January 1536. The specific charge was that the Queen had promised to marry one of her lovers once the King was dead. Norris was the particular target, Anne opening herself to this charge by admitting the exchange with him on 29 April when she teased him about 'waiting for dead men's shoes', in other words, the King's own death, so that Norris could then marry her.

Henry, during his reign, had always been paranoid about his tenuous hold on the throne, and had tightened up the original Treason Act of 1352 so that even to speak of the king's death could be interpreted as conspiring to the same. The notable thing about this is that when Anne was arrested none of these events on which she was tried was known—Anne only revealed the substance of her altercation with Norris on or after 2 May, while already in custody in the Tower. The normal sequence of events—suspicion, investigation, and finally an arrest—was not to be found. The arrest came first, then the Crown looked for the evidence.

Cromwell knew there would be no defence counsel; there would be no examination of the evidence. All that mattered at a Tudor trial was that due process was followed. The whole thing was a sad farce. Indeed it is not possible to determine why William Brereton was among the accused at all—there is no record of any evidence being given against him, and he was not a prominent figure in the Boleyn faction at court. It is suggested that he had crossed Cromwell over an entirely different matter, so Cromwell cynically swept him up with the others simply to get rid of him.

What should have been a further fundamental problem for the prosecution should not be overlooked. For a queen in England at this time to commit adultery was extraordinarily difficult without the collusion of at least one of her ladies-in-waiting. There was no privacy day or night—they shared Anne's suite of rooms. It is known that Henry's fifth wife, Catherine Howard, did indeed commit adultery, but to do so she had such an accomplice—Jane Rochford, George Boleyn's widow. She duly confessed and both queen and accomplice went to the block. But none of Anne's ladies–in-waiting testified in court against her.

Accounts of life in Anne's rooms do portray a lively social scene—certainly there was much dancing, including, as the trial was keen to point out, Anne dancing with her brother George. Furthermore, the trial was told in an effort to demonstrate that brother and sister had an unnaturally close relationship, Anne had written to George to tell him she was pregnant—and had exchanged a kiss with him. But neither of these things should have raised any comment—even the kiss. In strange contrast to current culture, the 16th-century French men and women marvelled at the English tradition of kissing when greeting. The Crown was struggling to make its case.

If Anne was guilty of anything it was of not keeping a sufficiently regal distance from her subjects. She was a vivacious, talkative person, who had an intelligent, inquiring mind; a woman of natural high spirits. It seems she allowed some adverse comment about Henry's wardrobe, his talents as a poet, and, worst of all, his virility. Unwise as some of her comments might have been (and it is ironic that Anne stumbled on her strong point—that of being able to say just the right thing at the right time), none of this amounted to treason.

Where was the smoking gun the prosecution looked for? Where was the needed accomplice for the charge of adultery to be credible? Many were prepared to tittle-tattle, but nobody could be found who was prepared to perjure him or herself against Anne. If anybody wanted, or indeed needed, to believe Anne guilty, it was the imperial ambassador—eager to please his emperor and get the 'concubine' replaced by Jane Seymour. Instead the worldly-wise Chapuys saw the trial for what it was—a farce.

Henry was a capricious and a vicious monarch. He could be ruthless with those who had served him well. Estimates vary as to how many he executed in his reign of thirty-seven years, but it certainly was not fewer than 50,000 people. He had by now made his mind up: he wanted Jane Seymour and there was no going back. He had even made arrangements that Anne should be executed by a Frenchman, an expert in the use of the heavy continental sword—the timetable of events suggesting that the executioner was ordered before the trial was finished. The French executioner could cut through the neck of victims in one swipe while they kneeled upright, rather than the traditional English way: the victims prostrate, with their head on a block.

During her time in the Tower Anne must have been under huge pressure. Not only was she facing her own gruesome death, she also believed that her own words, no matter how innocent, had somehow contributed to the death of her brother and others close to her. After the death of the men on the Wednesday it would be only natural if Anne considered what, if anything, might happen to save her. Perhaps Henry would relent; perhaps he would send her to a nunnery, as he had suggested to Catherine. It is said she recalled the happy times with Margaret of Austria. Nothing is revealed of what she said about Elizabeth, who was less than three years old, although Anne did express concern about her mother and father. It was a real possibility that all of her immediate family would be dragged down with her.

Even between her trial and execution the political manoeuvrings against Anne did not stop. On Tuesday 16 May Archbishop Cranmer visited Anne in a pastoral capacity and some believe he was asked to persuade Anne to sign away her marriage to Henry, in return either for a promise that she might be allowed to live, or for some assurance about Elizabeth's future safety.

Whatever transpired, on Wednesday 17 May Cranmer annulled the marriage, and so made Elizabeth illegitimate. In the July after Anne's death, the Second Succession Act was passed which stated that the King's marriage to Anne was indeed invalid. It appears that, in the convoluted logic of the time, Henry was able to justify this by saying that his previous relationship with Anne's sister Mary was the problem, despite Pope Clement VII having provided a dispensation for this specific situation. Henry now decided that this dispensation was like the previous pope's dispensation enabling him to marry Catherine—that it was against Scripture.[8] He could not have sexual relations with two sisters—no matter what the Pope said; divine law could not be the subject of a papal dispensation. The effect of this was a somewhat Alice in Wonderland scenario. If Anne was never Henry's wife, she could not have committed adultery, and she was entitled to make plans to marry Norris. This retrospective legislation effectively said that Anne was innocent as charged. But the legislation was not directed at Anne, but at Elizabeth. Both Mary and Elizabeth were now illegitimate, meaning that Henry's illegitimate son by Elizabeth Blount, Henry Fitzroy, stood to inherit the throne. Failing that, any offspring Henry had with Jane Seymour would be next in line, and, failing that, Henry in this Act had made provision for appointing his own successor. But within days of the Act being passed, Fitzroy died at the age of just seventeen.

In the end Anne seems to have come to terms with her fate, discussing with Kingston the actual details of the execution. He said, 'I have seen many men and also women executed and that they have been in great sorrow, and to my knowledge this lady hath much joy and pleasure in death.'[9] She expected to die on the morning of Thursday 18 May, the day after the others, and at dawn took Mass. She was witnessed swearing twice on the bread and wine that she had never been unfaithful to the King. Then, to her distress, she learned she was not to die until noon. In fact, it was not to be that day at all—the Friday had been set for the execution. How this misunderstanding arose is not known—it could be that when Anne heard of the annulment of her marriage she simply expected that the next day she would die. To comfort her in this time of distress she was told the execution would not be painful. Anne replied, 'I heard say the executor was very good, and I have a little neck.'[10] She put her hands round her throat and laughed.

Later the next day, on the Friday, she was taken from her rooms to Tower Green. She was escorted by Kingston and four women as she walked the final fifty metres. The scaffold was just a metre high, draped in black. There were 1,000 spectators there to see the first English queen to be executed. Among them were many Anne knew, including Thomas Cromwell himself. Following convention she moved to the edge of the scaffold to address the crowd. It is not known whether she had heard of her brother George's speech just two days before, but hers echoed the same sentiments:

Good Christian people, I have not come here to preach a sermon; I have come here to die. For according to the law and by the law I am judged to die, and therefore I will speak nothing against it. I am come hither to accuse no man, nor to speak of that whereof I am accused and condemned to die, but I pray God save the king and send him long to reign over you, for a gentler nor a more merciful prince was there never, and to me he was ever a good, a gentle, and sovereign lord. And if any person will meddle of my cause, I require them to judge the best. And thus I take my leave of the world and of you all, and I heartily desire you all to pray for me.[11]

How could she bring herself to describe Henry as a merciful prince? Convention demanded it, but, more importantly, Anne feared a backlash against Elizabeth and did not want to make matters worse. But there was no confession of guilt. By all accounts Anne was in control of herself; she spoke calmly and died boldly.

As was the tradition Anne forgave her executioner and paid him to do his work well. Her outer garment was removed revealing a low collar, giving an uninterrupted path for the sword. What was going through her mind at this time can only be imagined. Was she right to reject the system of the Roman Catholic Church, and instead throw herself directly on Christ's mercy? Within seconds she would know. The year before, Erasmus had written for her father Thomas Boleyn *A Preparation to Death* which Anne had probably read: 'In peril of death, man's infirmity is overpowered unless instant by instant, unless with a pure affection, unless within an unvanquished trust he crieth for the help of him which only reviveth the dead.'[12]

Anne simply kneeled down; she was not bound as was the way in Europe. Although calm, she did what so many others did in this situation and continually glanced behind, afraid that the swordsman would strike before she was ready. Over and over again she said, 'Jesus receive my soul; O Lord God have pity on my soul.' One of the ladies moved forward and tied a blindfold. Anne began to say, 'To Christ I commend my soul ...', and while her lips were moving the sword struck. All contemporary accounts agree that the executioner did his job well. It was over. We can only believe that her fervent prayer was answered: that as the cannons fired announcing her death, her soul was even then with Christ—which, as the Bible says, is 'better by far'.[13] Archbishop Cranmer was in the gardens of Lambeth Palace; on hearing the cannons he sat down on a bench and wept.

The ladies-in-waiting went quickly to the body and wrapped it in white sheets that rapidly stained red. Unaided, they carried the Queen the sixty metres into the chapel of St Peter ad Vincula, past the two new graves of Norris with Weston and Brereton with Smeaton. Her body was placed in an elm chest and buried in the chancel of the chapel.

In a display of fallen human nature, those at court were like vultures feeding on a carcass. All of Anne's forfeited property and income, and that of the other victims, was now booty to be fought over, and Henry's favourites competed for their share. Ignorant of the fate that awaited them, members of the victorious faction were jubilant. The woman who had such influence over the King with her reforming ideas was dead. In could come the old order of things. The Church could go back to its rituals, the Pope in his rightful place.

But first a wedding. On the very next day Henry was betrothed to Jane Seymour and they married at Whitehall on 30 May. Within the week members of her family were picking up honours suitable to their new-found status as relations to the King. Then came Cromwell's volte-face. He was not an aristocrat, neither was he part of the Church hierarchy. Power for Cromwell lay not in going back to the past, but in his relationship with the King. Those who got between him and that power were an obstacle. He had removed the biggest obstacle of all: Anne Boleyn; anybody now who looked to fill that vacuum was in danger. Cromwell knew the Seymours were there to stay, but others who had supported him in his coup would now be looking for favours; they needed to be dealt with. It was not the pay-off they expected.

One of the rewards the conservative faction hoped for was the full acceptance of Mary and her claim to the throne. But this is not what Henry wanted. Cromwell managed to convince the King that the reason for Mary's obstinacy in not simply acquiescing in her fate lay with her supporters. Backed by the King he started his second purge—two of Mary's supporters were excluded from the Privy Council and another, Lady Hussey, was put in the Tower. Others were interrogated by Cromwell, and anyone considered a suspect had to swear allegiance to the established succession.

This took the wind out of Mary's sails. She succumbed to the considerable pressure and signed away her right to the throne as Henry wanted. Now at last she must have realized that the prime mover in excluding her from the succession was her own father—not, as she had always surmised, Anne Boleyn.

Notwithstanding this victory Cromwell pressed on, and despite repeated denials from those he questioned he managed to get enough evidence to press charges of conspiracy—evidence far more credible than anything he ever had against Anne. This time, however, there was no need to take things to a final gruesome end: the relevant people caved in under pressure and were no longer a force to be reckoned with at court. Cromwell had won a great victory for Henry and was duly rewarded, as expected. In July Anne's father had to hand to Cromwell the office of Lord Privy Seal, and the next week Cromwell was given a peerage. Thomas Cromwell had achieved what he had set out to do in a remarkably audacious double coup. He had removed the Boleyn faction and then neutered the conservative faction; emerging from the carnage, both political and actual, with a powerful office of State and a peerage, the closest man now to the centre of power.

A consequence of Cromwell's cynical purge of the conservative faction, whether intended or not, was that the prospects for the furthering of biblical Christianity in England were significantly enhanced. If the conservatives had gained power undoubtedly it would have meant the end of religious reform and a return to medieval Catholicism. There was still some support for Mary at court, and popular support in the country manifested itself in rebellions in Lincolnshire and the north. Cromwell could not relax; over the next few years several of Mary's supporters were executed.

What drove Thomas Cromwell? Was his second purge to protect the political and religious reforms he had played a part in? If so it is unlikely he was seeking to protect the true spiritual nature of religious reform; looking back at the events it is difficult not to see that his real motivation was to enhance Thomas Cromwell—his influence, his power, his wealth. That certainly was the outcome, and Cromwell seemed pleased with it.

Yet God's Word does not speak in vain when it says: 'The one who sows to please his sinful nature, from that nature will reap destruction.'[14] Just four years later, on 28 July 1540, Thomas Cromwell was dead, sent to that executioner's block at the Tower of London by his beloved Henry. He had been falsely convicted, ironically, on a confusing mixture of rumour and innuendo. It is said that Henry VIII deliberately chose an inexperienced executioner, a young boy, who made three attempts at severing Cromwell's head before finally succeeding. The head was boiled and set on a spike on London Bridge—facing away from the City of London, the scene of his 'triumphs'.

Notes

1 **Starkey,** Six wives: the queens of Henry VIII, p. 578.
2 Quoted by **Ives,** The Life and Death of Anne Boleyn, p. 340.
3 **Starkey,** Six wives: the queens of Henry VIII, p. 579.
4 **Denny,** p. 299.
5 **Ives,** The Life and Death of Anne Boleyn, p. 364.
6 Ibid. p. 343.
7 Ibid. p. 343.
8 Leviticus 18:18, 'Do not take your wife's sister as a rival wife and have sexual relations with her while your wife is living.'
9 Quoted by **Ives,** The Life and Death of Anne Boleyn, p. 354.

10 Ives, *The Life and Death of Anne Boleyn,* p. 356.
11 Ibid. pp. 357–358.
12 Ibid. p. 358.
13 Philippians 1:23.
14 Galatians 6:8.

Part 3

Anne Boleyn's legacy

Anne in retrospect

The aftermath

Jane Seymour died in the year following her marriage to Henry, having given him the son he so longed for. Though Henry married three more times, no more children were born to him. After Anne's death, Henry's physical decline, portrayed so graphically in later paintings, set in. Furthermore he began to backtrack on some key elements of the Reformation; he was never an evangelical—he had supplanted the Pope's authority in England and that was sufficient for him. For example, in 1536 'The Ten Articles' were published with the King's specific authority—they were essentially Catholic in doctrine—and in 1538 he issued a ban on the importation of any book printed in English.

Henry VIII died in 1547 and Edward, his son by Jane Seymour, at just nine years old was crowned Edward VI; a council of regency took responsibility for government. They looked to consolidate the reforms of Anne's reign, but Edward died at the age of fifteen in 1553 and was succeeded by Mary, Henry VIII's daughter by Catherine. The following year the twenty-year-old Elizabeth, suspected of plotting a rebellion, was imprisoned in the Tower, just as her mother had been nearly eighteen years before. A two-month incarceration was followed by a year under house arrest. Mary reigned for five years and sought to reverse much of the Reformation in England, acquiring the nickname 'Bloody Mary' for the number of executions of those who opposed her Roman Catholicism. But in November 1558, at the age of forty-two, she died, and Anne Boleyn's daughter Elizabeth, as the new queen, was cheered into London by the crowds. In a reign that lasted nearly forty-five years she consolidated many of the Reformation teachings into national church life and doctrine.

What had Anne achieved?

History has been an essentially masculine affair, both in the key figures who made things happen, and in those who recorded it. Often the life and influence of a woman, for the purposes of a chronicler, was subsumed into the life of a man—be it her lover or husband. But history shows that Anne Boleyn played a key role in the Reformation in England, both as motivator and facilitator.

A BREAK FROM ROME

When Henry VIII ascended the throne, far from promoting reform, he opposed the 'new learning' that was sweeping into England from mainland Europe—and he was rewarded by the Pope for his stand against it. Neither did Anne Boleyn start the Reformation in England—it was Tyndale, along with many others, who laid the foundation for a new direction. But when the King was finally persuaded to put his weight behind the new teaching, defying Rome and appointing many evangelicals to key Church posts, the Reformation took on a new momentum. That persuasion came from Anne Boleyn, in the dynamic of her personal relationship with Henry. Her personal faith in Christ, her understanding of the 'new learning', and her desire to see it propagated propelled an often reluctant Henry down a path he would not have chosen for himself. In the opinion of several eminent historians today, if Henry had not had his change of heart, if he had not broken with the Pope in 1533, the future of England would have been the same as that of France—it would have remained a Catholic country.

A FUTURE QUEEN

Further, Anne gave birth to the daughter who, during her long reign, would consolidate the Reformation and see England known abroad as a Bible-loving nation. Although the reforms that Elizabeth oversaw were not as thorough as many would have liked, Elizabeth had the courage and political skill to push through changes that made Roman Catholicism no longer seem a viable option for the nation.

THE BIBLE IN ENGLISH

By the time Anne was queen the King's distaste for Bible translators had diminished and in 1535 Coverdale—a protégé of Tyndale—published the first complete Bible in English and felt secure enough to give it an unauthorized dedication to Henry VIII. Other Bible versions appeared, but it was the 'Great Bible' of 1539, with a preface by Cranmer, that became the official version. Although translated by Coverdale, there was considerable reliance on Tyndale's earlier translation.

Having the Scripture widely available in the vernacular was undoubtedly the key fact that secured the future for the English Reformation and over the years transformed English life. The Bible was freely available—and Anne played a key part in this. Hereafter kings and queens might come and go, but the Scriptures that Anne Boleyn had come to love were there for all to read. There on the pages of the Bible was the great doctrine of salvation by faith alone, through grace alone, based on Christ's completed work on the cross alone. There was no going back. The horse of English independence and love of the biblical gospel had bolted—and all efforts to lock the stable door by the Catholic Church were futile. There would be no widespread return to Catholicism, even with the bloodshed of Mary's reign. The Book of books in turn gave birth to Milton's *Paradise Lost*, Bunyan's *Pilgrim's Progress*, to the faith of the Puritans—the pioneers of New England who founded modern America—to George Whitefield, John Wesley, and the great 18th-century revivals.

WHAT ABOUT ANNE HERSELF?

In many ways 21st-century Christians find it difficult to relate to Anne Boleyn. Some see that she married a man in the process of a divorce and consummated her relationship with him before a valid wedding ceremony. But it has been shown that the vast majority of Christendom thought that Henry's marriage to Catherine was a forbidden marriage; what was disputed was the papal dispensation that enabled it to happen in the first place. Anne saw no basis for papal authority, so the dispensation, by definition, was invalid in her eyes. Even if it is believed that Anne was mistaken in marrying Henry, the fact remains that her mindset was that Henry was single—and all the evidence is that she went through a legitimate marriage ceremony that was perfectly acceptable in its day before consummating the relationship.

But despite these legal niceties should Anne not have seen the bigger picture? Henry and Catherine had lived as man and wife all those years, so they were surely de facto married in God's eyes. All the evidence points to the fact that she did try to stay away from Henry, certainly up until the gift of the model ship she sent him in July 1527, which Henry correctly took to be code that she would accept him as a suitor. Or was it all a game, and had Anne really been 'treating him mean to keep him keen'? Many new husbands, when relating how they courted their wives, proudly say how they pursued their intended and won her heart, only to learn later that they were following a road map the wife had conceived well in advance. It is surely true that most women have more guile in this matter than most men. Was this the case with Anne? Was Anne playing Henry along until he took the bait? But to what extent was it a realistic possibility at the time for Anne to turn Henry down? The leading authority on Anne Boleyn, Professor Eric Ives, thinks that Anne had little choice; Joanna Denny in her biography concurs; each reader will have to make up his or her own mind.

Another problem for some is not her intellect, but what might be considered to be the unfeminine way in which she used it. So unusual in her day, she was a self-made woman who moved and operated in a man's world. She had strong opinions and was unafraid of expressing them—often with a sharp wit and repartee. Undoubtedly she could at times be aggressive, which sits ill with a Christian profession.

And all that power dressing and extravagance? But 16th-century European monarchies largely modelled themselves on the Old Testament kings and queens, and Anne herself saw no tension at all between being a professed Christian and embracing the royal lifestyle that she did.[1]

Of course there were those flirtatious exchanges that played a part in her downfall—it is certain that Anne would have regretted them. And that unwise recommendation of her relative Eleanor Carey as the new Abbess of Wilton. Persons of influence were expected by their families to further their own—but Eleanor Carey was manifestly unsuitable for the post.

In mitigation of these criticisms it must be remembered that Anne Boleyn lived in very different times from our own. She owned only a small number of evangelical books; there were no Christian bookshops full of considered evangelical doctrine, no local Bible-based church to teach or encourage her, few people whom she could consider as mentors.

Events in Europe and in England were happening quickly and were frightening to many; all the old order seemed to be crumbling. There was no certainty that the 'new learning' would prevail—indeed in many countries it did not. There was fear of a backlash with drastic consequences at home and abroad; many evangelicals actually experienced violent opposition in France and elsewhere in mainland Europe, as also in England during the reign of Queen Mary. Anne swam against the tide of the Roman Catholic Church and other reactionary forces, in the process creating many enemies.

Anne made mistakes; some have come down through history, and there were surely others. I am certain that if she had been allowed the luxury of a retrospective view she would have done some, perhaps many, things differently. She was human, and showed her humanity and frailty when arrested and taken to the Tower. Who cannot have compassion on her for that? Any believer stands or falls before God based on his or her relationship to Christ. Those who are united to Christ through faith in him will be raised to life by him. Any judgement for believers will be based on how they have served their Saviour in the light of their own knowledge of Scripture and their conscience. Anne Boleyn, it appears, acted according to both.

Many Christians who have had biographies written about them would be disappointed if they were assessed on the first thirty-five years of their lives alone. For many this is the time when they are getting established and coming to settled beliefs; their most significant contribution would normally lie in the future. Anne really was a 'maker of history', and yet she was dead at the age of thirty-six, having served God's purpose for her life. Anne Boleyn was not alone—many made heroic stands for the gospel at this time and paid for it with their lives. But if Anne had not had the courage to take the gospel right to the heart of the Tudor court, it is unlikely that English national life would have been transformed in the way it was.

If there was the prospect of bringing any single person back from history to have a conversation with, then I would not choose the great apostle Paul, or Luther, or a famous Puritan: for my 'one-to-one' I would choose Anne Boleyn.

Note

1 See **Ives,** 'Anne Boleyn and the Early Reformation', p. 393.

Appendices

Recommended further reading

Joanna Denny, *Anne Boleyn* (Piatkus Books, 2004).

Eric Ives, *The Life And Death of Anne Boleyn* (Oxford: Blackwell Publishing, 2004).

David Starkey, *Six wives: the queens of Henry VIII* (London: Vintage, 2004).

Paul F. M. Zahl, *Five Women of the English Reformation* (Grand Rapids: Eerdmans Publishing Company, 2001).

The seven sacraments

There are seven sacraments of the Roman Catholic Church:

1 Baptism
People baptized according to the rites of the Church are freed from sin and reborn as sons of God.[1]

2 Confirmation
Strengthens the supernatural life received at baptism.

3 Eucharist
Known also as the Mass, or the Lord's Supper. When the bread and wine is taken Christ is re-presented to the Father. 'The Eucharist is not merely an image or symbol of Christ's sacrifice; it is Christ's sacrifice. The sacrifice of Christ and the sacrifice of the Eucharist are one single sacrifice.'[2] The bread and the wine truly become the body and blood of Christ, hence the Eucharist is to be worshipped—Pope John Paul II proclaimed: 'The Church and the world have a great need for Eucharistic worship.'[3]

4 Penance
Supplicants confess their sins to priests who 'by virtue of the sacrament of Holy Orders, have the power to forgive all sins'.[4] When sins are confessed to a priest 'the baptized can be reconciled with God and with the Church'.[5]

5 Marriage
The sacrament of marriage causes baptized Catholics to receive 'actual grace'.[6] The marriage bond is considered to be established by God himself and so is an indissoluble union.

6 Holy orders
'It confers a gift of the Holy Spirit that permits the exercise of a "sacred power" ... After ordination, a priest has the power to turn bread and wine

into the Body and Blood of Christ.'[7] 'Priests have received from God a power that he has given neither to angels nor to archangels.'[8]

7 Anointing of the sick

Also known as the last rites, in the 16th century it was called 'Extreme Unction' and was primarily performed when the recipient was close to death as a preparation for it. If the person 'has committed sins, he will be forgiven'.[9]

Notes

1 **Peter Kreeft,** *Catholic Christianity*, p. 308. This is an official publication of the Roman Catholic Church containing the *Nihil obstat* and *Imprimatur* verifications. Catholic doctrine has changed little over the years, although the Church has repudiated the abuses of the system seen in the late Middle Ages.

2 **Kreeft,** p. 327.

3 Quoted by **Kreeft,** p. 329.

4 **Kreeft,** p. 343.

5 **Kreeft,** p. 123.

6 **Kreeft,** p. 354.

7 **Kreeft,** p. 362.

8 Chrysostom, quoted by **Kreeft,** p. 123.

9 **Kreeft,** p. 374.

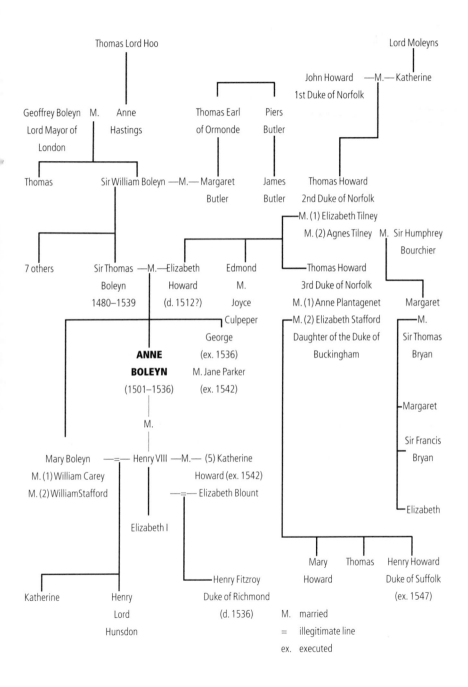

M. married
= illegitimate line
ex. executed

Biographical sketches

Catherine of Aragon, 1485–1536

Catherine was the youngest surviving child of Ferdinand II of Aragon and Isabella of Castile. In 1501 she married Arthur Henry VII's eldest son, but she was widowed within months. Then in 1509 she married Henry VIII, giving birth to Mary, the future Mary I of England, in 1516. Catherine's marriage to Henry was annulled in 1533 and she died on 7 January 1536.

Thomas Boleyn, 1477–1538

Anne Boleyn's father—alias Viscount Rochford, Earl of Wiltshire and Earl of Ormonde—was born at Hever Castle in Kent. He married Elizabeth Howard, who belonged to one of the leading aristocratic families of the day, her father, then in turn her brother, becoming the Duke of Norfolk. In contrast to the Roman Catholic Howards, Thomas Boleyn embraced the 'new learning' and became identified with the evangelical party. His eldest daughter Mary was for a time mistress to Henry before he married Anne. He was an able career diplomat and trusted advisor to Henry. Erasmus wrote a commentary for him on Psalm 23 and called him 'outstandingly learned'.

Eustace Chapuys, 1494–1550

He was the imperial ambassador to England from 1529 to 1536, that is, during the time of Anne Boleyn's rise, marriage, coronation, and fall. His significance is that much of what has been accepted in the past about Anne Boleyn came from his pen. But the reliability of his record of what was actually happening at court and the motivations for his accounts are open to question. His grasp of English was limited, so he was often fed information by others; and the Holy Roman Emperor, whom he represented, was the nephew of Catherine of Aragon—the Roman Catholic wife Henry 'divorced' for Anne Boleyn.

Thomas Cranmer, 1489–1556

He was born near Nottingham and studied at Jesus College, Cambridge.

He left to marry the daughter of a local tavern keeper, but when she died in childbirth he was re-accepted by the college and became a doctor of divinity in 1523. He came to the attention of the King in 1529 when he expressed the view that canon (that is church) law was not the same thing as the Bible, and that the solution to Henry's predicament over his marriage to Catherine of Aragon could be found there. He entered Henry's employment (also becoming personal chaplain to the Boleyn family) and was eventually appointed Archbishop of Canterbury. He soon made the long-awaited declaration that the King's marriage to Catherine was invalid and so could be annulled. He worked on a collection of doctrinal statements which form the basis of the Thirty-nine Articles of Faith of the Church of England. In 1556, during the reign of Queen ('Bloody') Mary and in the backlash against the Reformed faith, he was burnt to death at the stake, making a final heroic stand for the gospel after an earlier vacillation.

Thomas Cromwell, 1485–1540

He was a master politician, a student of Machiavelli, a Renaissance man of huge abilities. He became a key advisor to Henry VIII and embraced the new evangelical faith. Later, however, he dramatically turned against his evangelical friends and colleagues at court and became the architect of Anne Boleyn's fall. He was born the son of a blacksmith in Putney, but was an adventurer, fighting as a mercenary in Italy for the French, travelling widely in Europe and making a living as a trader. In Venice he became an accountant to wealthy merchants then made sufficient money trading in Antwerp to return to England to marry and study law. On his travels he had taught himself Italian, French, Latin, and some Greek. By 1514 he was a Collector of Revenues for the archdioceses of York and was soon working for Cardinal Wolsey, gaining his respect and becoming his principal secretary. On Cardinal Wolsey's fall he took his place as chief advisor to Henry, until himself incurring the King's displeasure. He was executed in 1540. Oliver Cromwell was descended from Thomas Cromwell's sister Katherine, who had married Oliver's great-great-grandfather Morgan Williams—the family adopting the Cromwell surname.

Henry VIII, 1491–1547

He succeeded his father Henry VII of England as king in 1509. He married six times: Catherine of Aragon (annulled), Anne Boleyn (beheaded), Jane Seymour (died), Anne of Cleves (annulled), Catherine Howard (beheaded), and Katherine Parr (survived). He broke with Rome and brought about the dissolution of the monasteries and the union of England and Wales.

Martin Luther, 1483–1546

A German monk and university teacher who, in October 1517, nailed on the door of Wittenberg Castle church a thesis containing ninety-five points against Catholic doctrine and practice—mainly its teaching about indulgences and the abuses which flowed from it. This proved to be a catalyst for the Reformation in Europe. He was a staunch proponent of the biblical gospel, particularly 'justification by faith', not works. His teachings, and those of others, were widely disseminated by the new printing presses of Germany, and fed the 'new learning' that came to England with, among others, Anne Boleyn.

Thomas More, 1478–1535

Born in London, he studied at Oxford, became a barrister and entered Parliament in 1504, becoming a member of the Privy Council in 1517. He was knighted in 1521. He became Lord Chancellor in 1529 after the fall of Thomas Wolsey. He was a fierce opponent of Luther. Although he supported Henry's divorce of Catherine in the House of Lords, in 1534 he refused to swear the 'Oath of Succession' to secure the succession of Elizabeth, Anne Boleyn's daughter. He was executed in 1535, and in 1935 he was made a saint in the Roman Catholic Church.

William Tyndale, 1494–1536

Born in Gloucestershire, he studied at Magdalen College, Oxford, and later at Cambridge. By 1522 he was noted for his 'new-learning' views, meeting at the White Horse Inn in Cambridge with like-minded friends. A gifted linguist, he had already determined to translate the Bible into English, meeting Luther in Germany in 1524. Following publication of his

New Testament in 1526 Cardinal Wolsey declared him a heretic and demanded his arrest; public burnings of his books were staged. Anne Boleyn showed Henry her (illegal) copy of his *Obedience of the Christian Man*; he was much influenced by it. Anne's copy of Tyndale's New Testament of 1534 is in the British Library in London. In 1536 Tyndale was tried and found guilty of heresy, executed by strangulation, and burnt.

Thomas (Cardinal) Wolsey, c.1473–1530

He was born in Ipswich, it is thought the son of a butcher. He studied at Magdalen College, Oxford, taking his degree at the age of fifteen. He became personal chaplain, first to the Archbishop of Canterbury and then to the governor of Calais (at that time an English territory), where he met Henry. In 1511 he became a member of the Privy Council (a small group of trusted advisors to the King), soon becoming its lead figure. He was made Roman Catholic Bishop of Lincoln and then Archbishop of York. In 1515 the Pope made him a cardinal and the same year he became Lord Chancellor presiding over the House of Lords and being a key government advisor. He enjoyed an extravagant lifestyle, living literally like a king at Hampton Court, maintaining a long-term mistress and fathering at least one child by her. His failure to secure the annulment of Henry VIII's marriage to Catherine of Aragon and his foreign policy mistakes caused him to fall out of favour with the King. He died of natural causes in 1530 on the way to an interrogation that probably would have led to his execution for treason. Few in the country, it appears, mourned his passing.

Bibliography

Budgen, Victor, *On Fire for God: The Story of John Hus* (Welwyn: Evangelical Press, 1983).

Cook, Faith, *Lady Jane Grey: Nine Day Queen of England* (Darlington: Evangelical Press, 2004).

Denny, Joanna, *Anne Boleyn* (London: Piatkus Books, 2004).

Dickens, A. G., *The English Reformation* (University Park, Pa.: Penn State Press, 1993).

Doran, Susan, *Elizabeth and Religion 1558–1603* (London: Routledge, 2004).

Dyer, Christopher, *Everyday Life in Medieval England* (London: Hambledon and London, 2000).

Dyer, Christopher, *Making a Living in the Middle Ages* (Harmondsworth: Penguin Books, 2003).

Edwards, Brian H., *God's Outlaw: The Story of William Tyndale and the English Bible* (Welwyn: Evangelical Press, 1976).

Elton, G. R., *Reformation Europe 1517–1559* (Oxford: Blackwell Publishers, 1999).

Foxe, John, *Book of Martyrs* (Grand Rapids: Zondervan, 1967).

Fraser, Antonia, *The Six Wives of Henry VIII* (London: Mandarin Paperbacks, 1993).

Gies, Frances and Joseph, *Life in a Medieval Village* (New York: Harper Perennial, 1991).

Guy, John, *Tudor England* (Oxford: Oxford University Press, 1990).

Haigh, Christopher, *English Reformations* (Oxford: Oxford University Press, 1993).

Haley, John W., *Alleged Discrepancies of the Bible* (Springdale, Pa.: Baker Book House, 1981).

Ives, Eric, 'Anne Boleyn and the Early Reformation in England: The Contemporary Evidence', *The Historical Journal*, 37/2, 1994.

Ives, Eric, 'The Fall of Anne Boleyn Reconsidered', *English Historical Review*, July 1992.

Ives, Eric, *The Life And Death of Anne Boleyn* (Oxford: Blackwell Publishing, 2004).

Kreeft, Peter J., *Catholic Christianity: A Complete Catechism of Catholic Beliefs Based on the Catechism of the Catholic Church* (San Francisco: Ignatius Press, 2001).

Marshall, Peter, *The Impact of the English Reformation 1500–1640* (New York: Hodder Arnold, 1997).

M'Crie, Thomas, *The Life of John Knox* (Glasgow: Free Presbyterian Publications, 1976).

Randall, Keith, *Henry VIII and the Reformation in England* (London: Hodder and Stoughton, 1993).

Rex, Richard, *Henry VIII and the English Reformation* (Basingstoke: Palgrave Macmillan, 1993).

Rosman, Doreen, *From Catholic to Protestant* (Abingdon: Routledge, 2005).

Saul, Nigel, *The Oxford Illustrated History of Medieval England* (New York: Oxford University Press, 1997).

Sheils, W. J., *The English Reformation* (London: Longman Group, 1989).

Starkey, David, *Elizabeth* (London: Vintage, 2001).

Starkey, David, *The Reign of Henry VIII* (London: Vintage, 2002).

Starkey, David, *Six wives: the queens of Henry VIII* (London: Vintage, 2004).

Warnicke, Retha M., *The Rise and Fall of Anne Boleyn* (Cambridge: Cambridge University Press, 1989).

Zahl, F. M. Paul, *Five Women of the English Reformation* (Grand Rapids: Eerdmans Publishing Company, 2001).

John Rogers—Sealed with blood
The story of the first Protestant
martyr of Mary Tudor's reign

TIM SHENTON

160PP PAPERBACK, 978–1–84625–084–2

John Rogers—
sealed with blood
The story of the first Protestant
martyr of Mary Tudor's reign

Tim Shenton

We in the west sorely need to craft a theology of martyrdom—it would put backbone into our proclamation and living, and help us remember brothers and sisters going through fiery trials even today in other parts of the world. Remembering men like John Rogers is a great help in the development of such a theology.
FROM THE FOREWORD BY MICHAEL HAYKIN, PRINCIPAL AND PROFESSOR OF CHURCH HISTORY AND REFORMED SPIRITUALITY, TORONTO BAPTIST SEMINARY, TORONTO, ONTARIO

Tim Shenton is the head teacher of St Martin's School and an elder at Lansdowne Baptist Church, Bournemouth. He is married with two daughters. He has researched and written extensively on church history, specializing in the eighteenth and nineteenth centuries. Among his works published by Day One are *Forgotten heroes of Revival*, *Our perfect God*, *Opening up 1 Thessalonians* and an expositional commentary on the prophet Habakkuk.

'Tim Shenton has produced yet another well-documented, gripping biography of a real hero of faith—John Rogers (d. 1555),

renowned biblical editor and first Marian martyr. Follow Rogers's fascinating career from Antwerp to Germany, and back again to England, where he was arrested, remained steadfast under intense interrogation, and paid the ultimate price for confessing Christ. This is a great book about an important epigone; hopefully, Rogers will no longer be marginalized! Highly recommended for teenagers and adults.'
—*JOEL R BEEKE, PURITAN REFORMED THEOLOGICAL SEMINARY, GRAND RAPIDS, MICHIGAN*

'Shenton weaves a brilliant tapestry from original sources and introduces the reader to many compelling and complex personalities. Well-proportioned in its emphasis, this history will be a vital contribution to studies of Protestant martyrs in Queen Mary's reign.'
—*RANDALL J. PEDERSON, CO-AUTHOR OF MEET THE PURITANS*